Amer

with the World

To My Sister & Brother:
Here's One way Americans act with others, as I
see it. Some aspects are praiseworthy. Some are not
but I believe that we've been the most civilized
of the choices so far.
My Love to you Both
Bob

ROBERT M. BROWN

University Press of America, Inc.
Lanham • New York • Oxford

Copyright © 2000 by
University Press of America, ® Inc.
4720 Boston Way
Lanham, Maryland 20706

12 Hid's Copse Rd.
Cumnor Hill, Oxford OX2 9JJ

Library of Congress Cataloging-in-Publication Data

Brown, Robert M.
America's way with the world / Robert M. Brown.
p.   cm.
Includes bibliographical references and index.
1. United States—Foreign relations. 2. United States—Foreign relations--
Philosophy. I. Title.
E183.7 .B698 2000   327.73—dc21   00-029863 CIP

ISBN 0-7618-1693-3 (pbk: alk. ppr.)

Contents

Preface

America's Way with the World is an account of the deep and stable motives which have shaped my nation's outlook on foreign relations, and consequent foreign policy, for over two centuries. I believe that the five American predispositions examined herein, in combination, provide our distinctiveness. I believe the five to be near immutable—forming a reliable framework for predicting the American's future global personality. The account is as unbiased a descriptive, explanatory and predictive analysis as this native son can make of his homeland.

I was politically socialized an American when my people were essentially united in and proud of our perceived global role—in the 1950s and early 1960s. At that time, checking and altering Soviet global intents seemed to be our most important task, and most foreign colleagues supported American leadership. Then, beginning in the mid 1960s, we Americans became divided and uncertain. In our Caribbean and Southeast Asian policies, some enemies were not totally "bad," and our friends were not totally "good." The direct and technology laden American approach in countering both foreign and domestic challenges often proved ineffective or counter productive. Our closest foreign colleagues increasingly favored alternative solutions to mutual problems, and they sometimes stood their ground. Yet, Soviet global imperialism was ended, and the old bipolar pattern which had organized the Cold War world came apart.

Unfortunately for us Americans, the genesis of a new pattern has not restored the domestic pride and cohesion which we held in the early Cold War period. We are divided over the relative importance of issues and the best paths to address them effectively. Many external challenges appear weakly responsive to our assets. We face poorly defined problems, not clear enemies. Our Cold War period associates are now true colleagues or peers, no longer clients to our preferred agenda. We Americans, at the millennium, if we are to regain our prior self confidence and policy stability, need a major change in outlook—one to match the major change extant in our surrounding environment. Henry Kissinger believes that America finally faces maturity—has finally reached that age when the nation must acknowledge that it is not very different in needs from any other nation. He believes that we have recently lost the special benefit of standing safely outside the global community of nation-states, offering an American constructed moral "beacon" and occasionally dipping in as a "crusader" for self selected causes. He believes that America "must at last develop and be guided by some steady definition of its national interest." We must acknowledge becoming just one more competitor, protecting our basic values domestically, and competing internationally for our share of this world's scarce resources.[1]

If Dr. Kissinger's explanation of America's disorientation and need is valid, knowing ourselves better—to include acknowledging our basic capabilities and limitations—must be an initial accomplishment. It is the stuff of successful environmental adaptation. Consequently, I intend this book to be partly a thoughtful "look-in-the-mirror" for my country's attentive public. For American university students of politics, it can be a beneficial contribution in American National Politics, International Relations and Comparative Political Systems core courses. It does as well fit in courses on American and Comparative Foreign Policy and International Political Economy. I intend it to stir discussion and put life into narratives about my people's international character.

America's Way is intended equally as reading for all foreign peoples who have an interest in knowing my country better. Understanding the stable motivations and consequent policy patterns of the globe's most influential state is essential for Asian and Mid Eastern professionals in business and government, hopefully fascinating for the curious European or Latin American student of world affairs. Use the model which I erect to sharpen your ability to engage my state and people effectively.

Certainly, *America's Way* contains unintended bias. Profiling a nation's character is a subjective undertaking, and all authors who analyze reality must rely on their individual paradigms to move their work forward. Yet, the book's content eases the task of unmasking that inadvertent bias. My position on long-debated issues is stated directly and clearly, and both the "Glossary of Terms" and the section "About the Author" provide grounding on my perspective. Mainly, I ask that you both critically read this book and plan to enjoy it. Think about its claims and conclusions, and then argue with friends and associates about the validity and reliability of my American paradigm. Above all, enhance your understanding of the beauty and ugliness which make us Americans, regarding us as another exclusive nationality trying to most beneficially fit in this complex global community. I wish you an engaging encounter with *America's Way with the World*.

Acknowledgments

In writing this book, the influences of three people have been invaluable to me. Russell J. Dalton, presently on the Graduate faculty at the University of California at Irvine, chaired my doctoral committee. His demanding yet sensitive and background rich tutorship added enormously to my ability to think constructively and write clearly in the fields of international and comparative politics. My beloved wife of four decades was born a West Berliner and socialized in both that divided city and London. Her unwavering support of my fascination with the politics of "the West" has provided the emotional encouragement necessary to author this book. I suspect that most writers need such an "intimate best friend" to stay the course to completion. Hristo Tenev attended the American University in Bulgaria and is now completing his degree work in journalism and politics at the University of South Alabama. This young Bulgarian scholar's extraordinary social maturity, sensitivity to his environment, experience beyond his years and commitment to improving the lot of his countrymen caused me to want his critical review of my draft manuscripts. His commitment to the request was total, and both his discrete challenge to some of my opinions and his suggestions on phrasing for undergraduate student consumption were invaluable.

Chapter I

The Setting

The Inevitable Climate of Change

I became politically aware in the 1950s—during the Truman and Eisenhower administrations. I claimed political adulthood during the "Camelot" years of John Kennedy. If you are in your teens, twenties or thirties, two huge differences probably separate your present outlook from the one which I held at your age. As an undergraduate student and a young professional, I believed that my material future was largely mine to make or break. By acquiring a baccalaureate credential, learning the essential occupational and social lessons offered through that program and applying those lessons diligently to my initial work, I would receive appropriate esteem and rewards. With substantial professional commitment, I could advance in my job to the level where I exercised direct policy influence. I could surely own that suburban home, two late model autos and a sport boat. Basically, my level of commitment and vocational contribution would govern my occupational and material rewards. If I considered some hurdles as "unfair", user friendly para legal and legal avenues would guarantee equitable reward for my efforts. My domestic political world was clear and unified—even if somewhat naive—in its promises, goals and values.

I was quite proud of America's global role. Through its initiative, Western Europe was being secured from Soviet influence and was regaining its economic health. The South Koreans were free from occupation by their North Korean kin because America had organized a multinational effort to block the aggressor's advances. Oh, our global image experienced temporary setbacks. The Russians orbited the earth before we did, and some policy muddle caused an American endorsed invasion of Castro's Cuba to fail. Yet, in the first case, we Americans knew that our superior research and development network would leapfrog over the Kremlin's challenge, using the Sputnik scare to energize our space and defense programs. In the second case, the Bay of Pigs invasion was not a wholehearted American commitment. Our security apparatus could always stop cold any major Communist adventurism in our hemisphere—as was confirmed in the outcome of the 1962 missile crisis. Unfortunately, some few Cuban "patriots" lost their lives or personal freedom in the failed invasion, but America's engagement was a complex global project. We were committed to physically walling in Soviet foreign influence while generating an improved life style for all people outside that wall. The small error at the Bay of Pigs was more than compensated for with the successful crystallization of global containment and the regional benefits promised Latin America by John Kennedy's Alliance for Progress. Yes, I served the Western cause proudly as a tank unit commander in late 1950s Berlin. Uniformity in our pride reinforced my officer colleagues' self assurance, and the all too visible East European alternative moved the citizens of West Berlin and West Germany to bolster—through their stated appreciation of our presence in their country— our self esteem. When I was a young adult the world was my oyster— both materially and ethically—because I was an involved American.

Now, a canyon of difference sits between your generation's outlook and mine when I was your age. You justifiably worry over prospects for establishing an emotionally and materially rewarding lifetime occupation. A baccalaureate often seems unmarketable, and any long-term vocational success, even if boosted through a graduate or professional degree, appears to depend largely on luck in avoiding personal impact from an industrial downsizing or an unexplained nationwide shift in economic conditions. Our less educated majority workforce senses even more catastrophic conditions: permanent job loss if their skill is expropriated by an offshore or foreign manufacturer, even loss of assurances for basic medical care with that job's evaporation. The suburban home, two auto and boat goal is too problematic to be worth contemplating.

More subconsciously, you question both the level of fairness in our legal system and the purposefulness of America's foreign policy. In high visibility trials, justice appears all too often compromised for other considerations. Celebrity status and jaded law enforcement seem to combine in delivering two legal codes—one for the special people and one for the rest of us. Legal processes following the deaths of Nichole Brown Simpson and the child model JonBenet Ramsey, plus criminal misconduct within our major metropolitan and some state police departments create your unease. America's foreign adventures tax and expend our resources with no apparent beneficial outcome or consistency of purpose: a short-lived involvement in Somalia, non specific benefit from our Haitian intervention, no end to our frictions with Saddam Hussein's and Fidel Castro's regimes and continuing involvement in Balkan ethnic problems which have festered for centuries.

Increasing alienation is one indication of our poorly defined but real and widespread dissatisfaction; again, you younger Americans being more detached and disappointed than is my generation. Yet, there is some good news. Most home grown alienation is not aggressive or strident. The incidence of an Oklahoma City type bombing or of disclosed plans for a self styled "militia" to release wanton social destruction is infrequent. Many of you young and early middle aged Americans merely regard public policy as somewhat meaningless in your lives or meaningful but generally controlled at levels shut out from your ability to influence. If disinterested, you merely become "non political". You don't even register to vote. If powerless, your frustrations manifest often as loosely targeted suspicion and quibbling across social subsets: male chauvinists versus feminists, laborers versus managers, pro-lifers versus pro-choicers, youth versus us older Americans. The resulting emptiness is reflected in our search for some common bonding—frequently along spiritual lines, with commitment to electronic evangelists or participation in mass morality events—the October, 1997 Washington rally of Promise Keepers or the responding gathering of women in Philadelphia.

The emotional detachment, social suspicion and personal insecurity pervasive among Americans are understandable. Over the four decades since I was an undergraduate, life in this country has changed enormously. Camelot ended with the assassinations of John and Robert Kennedy and Martin Luther King. Our never legitimated Vietnam conflict, the seamy nature of the Nixon administration's domestic politics and the intractable social pain caused by our ethnic and racial divisions brought us all to acknowledge the limits of our "special existence." Media attention has floodlit the egocentric side inherent in political ambition and the self-serving prejudices of our social structure. Yet, discovery that the American experience has created a no more sublime society than any preceding one—that the emperor still has no clothes—is easier for my generation to rationalize away than for generations who were being socialized at the time of discovery. I once knew an America whose status was not in question. My daughter never knew that America. She cannot reference a past that seemed uniquely successful, and consequently has less hope that it can exist. If you haven't been there, you can't hope to return.

A second, more global set of changes have added to the domestic whirlwind shifts of the late 1960s and early 1970s. Restructuring of the world's economic framework has diminished our hegemonic leverage and, with it, assurances of prosperity for most Americans. Additionally, the disintegration of our only credible enemy's empire has let loose a new set of international dangers—denying us the familiarity we had gained in handling old enemies. Our compass for identifying threat has gone. Details of the global economic rearrangement, and of the impact of substituting vague dangers for clearly defined enemies, will be addressed shortly. At this point, we need acknowledge only that global shifts in relations between states and a painful maturing of the American self image have left us justifiably disoriented as a nation—again, you younger Americans more so because you lack the recollection of any time when Americans were self assured.

You should recognize that massive environmental change always brings disorientation. You might consider our greatest danger to be a failure to grasp soon enough both the nature of the changes and the extent of our capabilities and limitations in adjusting beneficially. The remainder of this chapter describes in detail the major dimensions of those changes, as I understand them. Chapters two through six describe five deeply embedded American predispositions which shape our capabilities and limitations in addressing the current environment, and in my final chapter I've placed the five core American predispositions against our major domestic, foreign and system-wide challenges, offering probable near-term future outcomes as my country gropes into the early 21st century.

One enormous assumption underpins the weave of this book, and it stems from the optimism of my 1950s and early 1960s socialization. It is that we **will** restore a common belief in our society, an esteem as strong as the one I had when I was a young adult. It assumes energetic and stable reengagement of my country in the global community, certainly in a role quite different from the one which America practiced for its initial two and a half centuries, but in one still shaped by the five traits which have always shaped our national character. Our future, if my assumptions prove wrong and our present disorientation and internal divisions become established conditions, is a subject beyond the scope of this book. It is probably a tale of America's eclipse as a world power and as a place of public well-being. Robert Reich has profiled that future American society in his book, *The Work of Nations*. He presents the prospect of an openly divided society in which the minority, through advanced education and possession of complex skills, garners most of our sought after values while the majority are physically and emotionally warehoused, contributing little to the society and developing little self respect. That would no longer be a democratic America. Our soul requires widespread public well-being, influence and self-esteem. The Russian playwright Shatrov has depicted that other less fortunate type society. In *Onward, Onward, Onward* he has Rosa Luxembourg expose the necessity of citizen engagement. She exclaims, "Without general elections, without unrestricted freedom of the press and assembly, without a free struggle of opinion, life in every public institution dies out, becomes a mere appearance, and bureaucracy alone remains active."[1] The pitiable condition is fictionally portrayed through the oppressive life styles lived by Soviet citizens in the novels of Aleksandr Solzhenitsyn and Anatoly Rybakov.

Today's World

My youth's halcyon nature was substantially a product of America's post World War II hegemonic status. In 1944, at Bretton Woods, New Hampshire, we wrote the non Communist world's rules on international trade and finance. At the war's end, we stimulated and enforced those rules through our dominant economy, advanced technology and globally deployed military forces. America alone determined which friendly states would be revitalized first from the war's destruction, which would provide our foreign resources, and which would become markets for our finished commodities. We set price structures, selectively opened our coveted domestic market and enforced the Bretton Woods rules with a global network of military alliances responsive mainly to American interests. Why wouldn't my generation believe that the world was our oyster forever?

But, by definition, dynamic relationships change. Because the principal recipients of our massive postwar recovery programs had been industrial and trade giants before the war, they grew into friendly competitors. By the early 1970s, Japanese and German products equaled ours in quality and market appeal. Their currencies were as vigorous as was the dollar.

As additional allied states reestablished their production and trade competitiveness, and some new ones joined the community of advanced economies, America's position gravitated from dominance toward becoming just the most voluminous player. In addition, an entirely new pattern was being woven into the fabric of global manufacturing, trade and finance. Before the war, America domestically controlled its economic activity. A large and prosperous internal market plus a global market network not yet dominated by any one state assured us of that privilege. During the war, we became our allies' principal weaponry and foodstuffs supplier—a function which enlarged enormously our manufacturing and transport capacity and expertise. We then met the postwar recovery challenge by implanting permanently those assets globally. At the time, that policy provided both the most direct and most familiar means of support for our Cold War strategy. It also materially enhanced the American economy.

The unforeseen outcome was that, by expanding from an essentially regional to a global economic engagement, we erected a system which could only end in our loss of hegemony. We are now caught in the resulting oxymoron—"competitive interdependence." America's foreign based and her domestic activities are inseparable, and the resulting fusion reduces our leverage, frustrating autonomous control over our interests. Because every state's economic policy targets maximum domestic prosperity, America's fortune eroded as those of our competitive colleagues rose. While I was socialized in a transient period of reigning privilege, you are experiencing an end product leveling of the playing field. I had material expectations. Your outlook is not as optimistic.

The emotional impact of our changed condition runs deep and personal. When my country dominated the western world's economic activities, and policy served the perceived wants of Americans, it was a comforting simplification to separate domestic and foreign policy issues. We could make our foreign policy agenda largely serve domestic wants. Now, with our diminished state leverage and increased international bonding, foreign—other state—preferences and priorities frequently upstage ours. We have to compromise. Markets, manufacturing processes, access to resources, commodity research activities and ways of financing those initiatives are internationally shared; and since all local politics has become foreign politics, we can no longer place or meaningfully prefer domestic over foreign initiatives.

Europeans have known competitive interdependence for over a century. Geographic proximity and near equality in influence generating assets, any one to all other European states, assured that condition. Because each has needed external colleagues for some time, Europeans have come to accept a regionally mandated sense of limited state autonomy. We Americans, by singularly undertaking postwar restoration of the global economic network, unwittingly self selected the same status, eventually. That day has arrived, and its structure promises to be quite permanent.

We labeled our Bretton Woods way "the liberal international economic order." Ideally, state imposed barriers to the free exchanged of goods and services were to disappear—just as they had between our union of fifty united states. Each nation-state would then gravitate naturally toward producing, for the global market, those commodities and services in which it excelled. We established American manufacturing subsidiaries worldwide, hiring indigenous laborers and allowing some foreign regimes to establish and hire in our country. We let the dollar flow where it could most energize our corporate profits, and we spread American technical and managerial creativity. Within three decades, America's way with the world had fashioned a historically new global economic mosaic. There were, by the mid 1980s, no world spanning corporations which were truly American, or German, or Japanese or British or any other nationality. Our Bretton Woods creation established the 21st century's global structure because the process of creating it incorporated most every state in the world—many of them newly formed. It will be with us indefinitely because, unlike the more cosmetic stock (portfolio) ownership patterns of the prewar years, foreigners now exercise direct managerial influence in America's manufacturing and sales activity. It will remain because, unlike the prewar colonial pattern in which one parent state controlled vertically and exclusively the economies of a set of colonized states, international economic integration is now horizontal. The horizontal pattern emerges because the most advanced states now produce largely from indigenous resources and market their products well only with each other. No longer is Britain required to secure cheap rubber from Malaya, turning that rubber into finished products at home and returning those products to Malaya for sale at a profit. Britain now substitutes domestically produced synthetics for Malay rubber. Its sophisticated end products then sell well only within other advanced economies. As we advanced economies refocus activity among each other, our past colonies become aware that they are left out. The two layered horizontal pattern—the advanced and the disadvantaged communities of states—emerges. Many of the disadvantaged struggle to carve a place in the favored network. Challenges to their success are legion, fueling domestic frustration and regional instability. It makes for a very unstable world, doesn't it.

The current mosaic is deeply seeded also because capital—the fuel of contemporary global economics—has lost its national character. Activities of the Tokyo, New York, London and Frankfurt stock exchanges fuse all major business activities across those states. Again, this condition provides America with the partial leverage accorded the largest volume player, but it denies us our prewar managerial dominance and autonomy. While each major economy benefits from profitable financial initiatives of any one state colleague, none of us can allow others to suffer devastating losses because of the unknown consequences to our own interests.

The consequences of this last business linkage impact directly the individual American industrial worker—the Detroit welder in a General Motors assembly plant or the Valley, Alabama weaver in a WestPoint Stevens garment factory. While the investment capital supporting those two manufacturing processes can leave Michigan or Alabama for profitable reapplication in Mexico's Maquiladoro zone or Taiwan's Taipei, the Detroit and Valley workers are rooted. With capital mobile and labor fixed, is it surprising that American skilled labor and industrial lower-middle management sense job insecurity, that your employment prospects are often not as long-term predictable as were mine when I was your age?

Yes, insecurity and confusion run throughout our foreign policy views. There is no national consensus on end goals, and the consequent policy fluctuations seem to produce inconsistent and ill rewarded application of our tax dollars. Few Americans are convinced that our resources are being applied effectively against what threatens us most—whatever that is. Robert Art, a leading defense analyst, has given some definition to the source of our current disorientation over national security. He believes that in half a century America has traveled through two security environments and is now entering a third one. Before World War II, our physical security needs were clear in a "geopolitical" world. Four major European powers, Japan and a young America were counterbalanced players on a chess board where moves were for mutually understood purposes. At the war's end, only the Soviet Union and America had the resources and societal cohesion to continue the play. We two locked horns on ideologically incompatible goals, and with the limited maneuver available in that "bipolar" game, the rules of engagement became even more obvious. By the mid 1980s, the Kremlin regime's resources were exhausted and its ideology was discredited, both externally and at home. Its disintegration has now thrown the only remaining superpower into a wholly new and lonely gameplay—into an early 21st century world undergoing yet another political and economic mutation.

Art terms this third environment the "crazies" era.[2] Its seemingly schizophrenic logic was present but suppressed during the "geopolitical" and "bipolar" eras. While each of the six major colonizers and then either of the Cold War superpowers was forcefully extracting support and loyalty from its client states, the subordinated clients kept their domestic ethnic and religious grievances to themselves. During the prewar "geopolitical" era, each colonizer muzzled such grievances mainly to marshal uniformly the resources of its empire. During the postwar "bipolar" period, the requirement to suppress was placed even more strongly on Washington or Moscow. We two were entrapped in what was considered a globe spanning fight-to-the-finish. Soviet and American counter moves introduced weapons systems the initial use of which would surely escalate, with an ultimate outcome of tearing civilization asunder. The physical fear of extinction supersedes, in priority, all other fears. Consequently, we two prohibited our clients and supporters from exercising any autonomous force toward settling their long-standing grievances. We could not afford side show clashes which might escalate into a superpower faceoff—a potential of the end of civilized history, through miscalculation.

Now, with the more "rational" organizing principles of the geopolitical and bipolar eras gone, the patron state's control over its clients has evaporated, and long held hatreds and cross-cultural suspicions have resurfaced as the small states' primary agendas. The label "crazies" era fittingly describes this contemporary environment because two new ingredients provide a heightened danger in the long suppressed tribal, ethnic and religious frictions. First, the unbridled leadership of today's "causes" can credibly label the poverty endemic to their societies as a permanent and worsening status if basic interstate relationships don't change. They recognize clearly the growing gap in well-being between North and South, and want a system retooling to provide them with their fair share. We want them to have it, but not at our expense, and we do not know how to redistribute without personal disadvantage. Second, once invented and manufactured in quantity, the geopolitical and bipolar eras' weapons of mass destruction can neither be disinvented nor can their spread of ownership be absolutely blocked in a hate filled and frightened world. Your generations, my readers, face tough times because the long-held cross cultural vendettas, which generate many intrastate and interstate frictions, are backed by weapons arsenals of awesome lethality.

Yes, we are beginning to rewrite the books on how international relations work, but my generation's experience is in deflecting the highly visible enemies of the geopolitical and bipolar eras. Trident submarines kept the Kremlin's ambitions at bay, but are an irrelevant tool in settling the Balkans' ethnic vendettas. Stealth bombers have little use in dispelling the deep animosities nurtured by generations of Latin Americans toward what they label Yankee exploitation. The singular, external and concrete *enemies* which America once faced are supplanted by multiple, often system wide and definitionally illusive *dangers* to our way of life. As best we can, we must substantially renovate our outlook, our actions and the tools we use in dealing with others. Suddenly, a new basis for interstate relations makes preservation of my American values and well-being dependent on my peoples' ability to modify effectively America's outlook on and its way with the world.

Defining the Remedies

A national character is as much the result of a reactive response in accommodating unintended environmental stimuli as it is an overt action to stimulate new environments. America is unintentionally in but must get through the "crazies" era. My wish is that, in finding our way through, we regain the domestic commonality of outlook and goals, the cultural self esteem, the vocational optimism and sense of material well-being which I once enjoyed. My wish is that we build policy on a realistic understanding of what propels the crazies, on a realistic understanding of the limits of autonomous American initiatives, and on a clear acknowledgment that there are aspects of our American personality which we cannot change, but must deal with as limitations.

If my country's external dangers emanated solely from ignorance of or indifference to extant inequality in well-being between nations, temporary adjustments to start the less advantaged nationals on an improved path might be feasible. On a cost-benefit basis, we affluent societies might consider any temporary material setbacks experienced by making asset transfers as less painful than the consequences we would face from building hostilities as we stonewalled our advantage. If the imbalance in wealth between states were between like minded cultures, the transfers might even relieve us of some guilt by having rectified past abuse of our "kin." Certainly, we could anticipate the use of the transferred assets because the new owners would apply them much as we had done, to achieve—by our standards—some permanent level of improvement in well-being.

But the external dangers are only partly the result of acknowledged disparity in well-being and influence in controlling its flow. The past colonial powers, America uniquely prominent among them, are materially advantaged largely because our national values fuel that rewarding economic structure. A symbiotic relationship exists between successfully developing and managing the contemporary globally competitive economy and applying three cultural preferences. Those preferences are national commitment to a pluralistic—non authoritarian—social structure, to a secular—non fatalistic or theocratic—way of controlling one's destiny and to internally competitive—non ascriptive—criteria for choosing leadership. National modernization will be stunted midway in its development, capping public well-being, in societies caught within authoritarian social structures, steeped in theocratic or faith based approaches toward self improvement and accepting of leadership chosen on any basis other than secular proven ability to lead effectively. Most materially disadvantaged nations currently have and will cling to one or more of those economically debilitating value outlooks. Domestic socialization—habit—has made those hampering values comfortable props for large indigenous subcultures, and they will resist losing their props. They want the well-being of the prosperous West without adopting its means of getting and keeping that prosperity.

Because economic development and social modernization require the changing societies to hold modern outlooks, rapid development and modernization destabilize most traditional societies as old props of social interaction are swept away. The disoriented public feels naked and non specifically threatened by surroundings which it did not request or anticipate. The reaction can be civil war, a plunge back to the old and established ways, and self chosen regional isolation—as it was with 1970s Iran. It can be a peaking of development as old values cripple change, followed by public frustration over unrealized expectations, and a fracturing of the state's authority. Social and economic disarray within the defunct Soviet Union is illustrative. Consequently, poorer nations remain aware of their poverty, determined to rectify the imbalance, but ill prepared to adopt those value structures which fuel successful development programs currently. As with Iran and the Soviet Union, their domestic failures will inevitably impact us through regional and global instability. Because American prosperity depends heavily on stable global conditions, we will continue to absorb—through damage to our own well-being—the growth pains of aspiring societies frequently led by "crazies" and responding to what we consider crazy causes.

The attitude change in Americans must be experienced by more than that tiny percentage of us who professionally deal in policy making and execution. My country will not adapt to the new, endangering conditions if only that small subset gains a new perspective. We Americans function well only as a true participant society, with our policy makers and keepers constantly sensitive to and guided by what they believe to be their constituents' wishes. Both electoral insecurities and institutionalized openness to competing interest group pressures keep American leadership representative—and somewhat validate the label "democracy." Alexis de Toqueville, the 19th century Frenchman who developed a love-hate mesmerism with American society, identified the fuel of our dynamic cohesion. He regarded us to be a society built and held together by the force of a "collective **self** interest."

If the demands of America's widespread community of grassroots activists are based on passe or ignorant perceptions of our world, our leaders will be chosen with a flawed view of our needs. The voters' mistaken belief that the foreign and domestic agendas debated in our 1996 Presidential race were separable is an example. George Bush's concentration on trade with Japan and on assuring the easy availability of Middle East oil for our trading partners' usage were as critical in protecting American jobs and purchase power as was any domestic activity he could have undertaken. The President can service domestic needs only by pushing both foreign and domestic agendas, not by withdrawing from the former to more emphasize the latter. Alternatively, if our sensitive electorate, from frustration over dealing with the complexity of current dangers or for other reasons, turns its energy and attention away from hammering out well structured demands on the Capitol and White House, our presidents and legislators will act with uncertainty as to their mandate or timidity as they execute only vaguely legitimized policy. Early in its first term, the Clinton administration recognized that economic challenges had supplanted, in importance, challenges to our physical security. Over the previous half century, as factors in the Cold War made physical security our paramount concern, we had evolved a very successful organizational structure for orchestrating military policy—the National Security Council (NSC). The Clinton White House created a similarly fashioned National Economic Council (NEC) to address the new priority. Yet, that executive leadership did not forcefully relegate the NSC to a narrowed role by insisting on functional acceptance of its new creation. With no clear public mandate, the White House initiative was timid, and the Congress responded largely through either internal division or protection of Cold War vested interests. The NEC initiative withered.

Yes, our future well-being depends substantially on how well the United States citizenry learns the advantages of team play, respecting national differences and understanding the logic of others' dislike of us. We can no longer blame the Kremlin's venality for troubles between America and Castro's Cuba or other, only marginally more friendly hemispheric regimes. My country's bonding into a global pattern of competitive interdependence will not be threatening if we understand and work with that pattern's character. As our world is composed of over 180 nation-states, each claiming ultimate sovereign control over its people, we must become comfortable with applying two quite different codes of conduct simultaneously. We Americans are among the most ardent protectors of our autonomy, and autonomous planning and administration are beneficial where issues remain domestic in nature. Yet, sovereignty at home mandates the absence of a sovereign spanning the 180 state community. We must learn to listen and accommodate, where feasible, in our dealings with the world beyond America. We must become better "team players" out of respect for the recent equalizer bestowed on small states through modern weapons proliferation and those states' control over resources which we need. The need is not that my country become timid, but that necessarily assertive relations include our sincere acknowledgment of other states' disadvantaged domestic status and our equally sincere willingness to cooperatively work through differences between us.

Yes, you younger Americans are more upset than I am over America's new lot. Yet, your stronger emotion may be a more promising outlook for improving our future. My generation's greater complacency is built on past and now largely irrelevant or inappropriate perspectives. You do not have to unlearn what are now bad habits. You young and early middle aged Americans may well develop a constructive approach to the contemporary world before my Cold War associates do. We have vested interests and habitual application to shed. Realistically, our experience and your energy must combine to "find the middle ground between abdication and overextension," as Henry Kissinger so concisely phrased the new approach which America must seek.[3]

The Limits of American Flexibility

Gabriel Almond and G. Bingham Powell consider political culture to be the pattern of attitudes, opinions and beliefs which we hold about our political environment.[4] Those two scholars have clearly demonstrated the controlling influence of a national culture on its adherents' lifestyle. Culture implants the lenses which color all that we comprehend, framing the questions we ask, the interpretations we place on responses to those questions, even determining the policies we erect and the outcomes we expect from them. The dimensions of a national culture are developed over centuries of learning, and remain unique to that nationality because its learning experiences have been unique. Culture is transmitted from generation to generation through the institutions which socialize a society. My cultural mosaic makes me think and act as an American.

Partly because a culture is so long in the making, partly because we act within cultural boundaries and on cultural preferences and priorities without full awareness of the channeling taking place, partly because constant association within our common cultural environment reinforces that culture's stability, partly because our institutions not only stabilize our cultural web but are themselves stabilized by its consistency, culture is extremely resilient. Oh, the functions of institutions change as a state's larger environment evolves. The American political party structure exercised a stronger policy making role in the 1920s than it does today, but only because the two party structure was the best available representation of labor's and management's competitive goals. Factory labor was based on the assembly line, and the northern Democratic party could expediently represent labor's uniform drive for improved wages and benefits. In like manner, the entwined interests of those who owned and managed our factories, railroads, shipping companies and banking interests were able to aggregate their actions through the Republican party. Today, the socio-economic distinction between the agendas of labor and management is not neat—in the electronics, computer software and hardware and other high and medium technology and many service industries for example. The percentage of our workforce with occupations which latch to an assembly line has diminished, and the consequent influence of that "smokestack" industry's contribution to our economic health has declined. Additionally, ownership, management and finance are much less purely American than they were in the 1920s. Consequently, a major segment of labor and management—the foreign based segment—finds the American party structure irrelevant to realizing its goals. Today, American laborers and managers gain more leverage on policy through support of specific interest groups: Chambers of Commerce, Rotary and Kiwanis Clubs and a host of vocation specific interests. But this shift in institutional influence—from party structure to interest network—is merely a shift in tools. Culturally, the American of the 1990s remains the American of the 1920s—an individualistically competitive and self serving citizen. Only the instrument which serves that self serving competitiveness has changed—from party system to interest network.

Consider, for a moment, how nationalities are stereotyped. In quick judgment, other people regard the Germans—by *nature*—as "industrious," "loyal to their superiors" and quite "assertive as a nationality." Certainly, their postwar economic recovery, recent success in unifying their eastern and western sectors and present domestic prosperity support that century old stereotype. The experiences of defeat in one world war, regime destruction and military occupation in a second, and forty years of division and control by two ideologically opposed superpowers have not altered those resilient cultural characteristics. What better test of the staying power of a national culture than the tests faced by the 20th century German culture? What stronger testimony to the personality forming role of culture than that we use its identification in describing a nationality or tribal community? Industry and assertiveness developed as German characteristics because the Germans were influenced by the Italian Renaissance movement, contributed centrally to the anti-Catholic Reformation, were leading contributors in both the 17th century "age of reason" and 19th century western ideological development. Geography and the spread pattern of Eurasian civilizations forged the Germans' tendency toward collective effort and national assertiveness. German borders did and do offer no topographic barrier to physical or cultural invasion—no difficult to traverse mountain ranges or oceans. Thus, Germany became the anvil on which the Gaelic, Roman, Slavic and Scandinavian armies and cultures hammered each other for supremacy.

Consequently, Germans acquired the need to persevere together because only such a tight knit and determined outlook could have maintained self identity in the face of Roman, Slavic, Napoleonic and Nordic influences.

Conversely, stereotyping labels the average Russian as politically indifferent, superstitious and far more covetous of the family circle than of any nationality or state construct. Those characteristics were again centuries in the making. Russia's vastness was, to Russian society, both a blessing and a curse. While offering a protective buffer against the military adventures of West European empire builders, it inclined the Russians to remain a peripheral, backwash people as western European societies modernized. The Renaissance, the Reformation and the liberal Enlightenment only marginally penetrated Russian society. The industrial revolution came late to that vast agrarian nation at the unprofitable edge of established trade routes, and a frigid climate further hindered industrial growth. In order to extract any support from its impoverished people, Russian authority was centralized—the Russian Orthodox church being subordinated to both the Czars and the Bolshevik leadership. The Enlightenment's code that authority over a populace bears reciprocal responsibility to that public did not take root in Romanov or Soviet leadership. Consequently, except in time of national threat, state authority remained mainly indifferent to the individual Russian's well-being. Left to fend for itself, the Russian family alone nurtured a "civilized community", and the formalized powers in Moscow—because their only contacts were viewed as negative—were suspect and to be passively avoided.

We Americans formed our unique character from yet a third set of circumstances. Our colonial founders were very individualistic, religiously guided and materially ambitious. Seldom drawn from the elite classes in their native countries, they were both persevering in their material ambition and suspicious of authority. Those traits combined to propel America toward its 1776 Revolution. Those traits assured us of a very representative group as we erected our public leadership. The American Constitution has remained our governance polestar for over two centuries because its content defines the core of the American character. That document's horizontal division of authority between three competing branches of government and vertical division of authority between the national and state governments and the people testify to our distrust of any authority— near delusionary fear of concentrated state power. The daring uniqueness of its regime structure reflects clearly our certainty of American "exceptionalism," and the honored role carved for the citizen declares the value we place on and the potential we believe to be in the individual. There is little respect offered to our pre Constitutional experiences, but a continuing undertone of adherence to a universal moral code is apparent. An expressed preference for guidance through a self styled moralism--as opposed to hereditary, secular experience—is pure Americana. The American Constitution is saturated with conditions for the conduct and protection of private business activity, a focus which fits our devotion to both an unfettered marketplace and material acquisition.

Until the mid 20th century, we Americans perceived no advantage in undertaking a permanent global managerial role. But requirements and outcomes of our wartime activities, and the mid century collapse of the international imperialist system, compelled us to unify international relations throughout the non communist world under one postwar design. That design essentially mirrored the American cultural map, and it became the standardized Cold War means of Western international interaction. Now, with disintegration of the Kremlin's empire, some Western trading institutions and processes are being adopted globally. The irony of this development is that, although the pattern was fashioned from America's cultural makeup, its widespread adoption institutionalized our continuing commitment to its formulas without a guarantee that America would always hold controlling influence in its activity. Our current loss of direction is a by-product of America's slippage in control over that largely cloned environment.

Individual disorientation and insecurity caused by a changing social environment has been termed "cognitive dissonance." Again, when afflicted with this challenge, any national culture tends to seek emotional stability by clinging to culturally familiar codes which have worked successfully in the past. True, the probability is that old remedies, whose success rested on old environmental conditions, wont succeed in the new environment, but the regression is an emotional defense, not a rational one. America's current funk is a mild case of cognitive dissonance. Our regressive choice is to continue applying the policies of the Cold War period. They worked well for us previously, and we do not yet know what else to do. Until the engaged American public reaches some consensus on a new, best policy agenda, those largely inappropriate Cold War approaches will be used. They have the comfort of familiarity and the staying power attached to a previous leadership community's protection of its vested interests.

The remainder of this short book is my description and explanation of five cultural dimensions which have and will continue to determine both the goals and style and the flexibility limits of America's adaptive agenda. Liken the five, in combination, to the shape of a human body, and America's Cold War policy set and the replacement set which we will need in the 21st century to two different suits of clothing. By acknowledging our body shape and size—the shape and size of our five cultural dimensions—I offer an interpretation of both the possibilities and some probabilities in future attire—of both continuance and modification in policy agenda. The sooner we dress to fit—play to our cultural strengths and limits—the sooner we will be reclothed to our benefit. Chapters 2 through 6 describe the five characteristics separately, offering some explanation of each trait's background. The last chapter offers a mosaic of how the five fuse in today's world.

In Chapter 2, I look at how political, economic and social life in America are shaped by our core drive to satisfy individual self interest. Uniquely, we treasure the Lochean value of satisfying the individual first. Chapter 3 centers on our "present centered" nature. Custom, heritage and tradition are far less important in an American's determination of what to do next than is common in any other advanced society. Chapter 4 explains how past successes and geographic advantages have nurtured in us a preference for solo solutions to challenges. We abnormally shun arrangements in which we cannot control absolutely the evolution of policy. Chapter 5 describes the extent to which we are "children of the world." Again geography, but also the processes by which America grew to a continental sized superpower, have made us more self assured—often wrongfully—of our ability to deal with all races and ethnic groupings than are most other nationalities. In Chapter 6, I demonstrate how home grown morality is a more influential determinant of what we do as a nation than it is or has been with most world powers. We openly and sincerely apply an American developed code of ethics universally to our every foreign policy action.

I believe that the combined interplay of those five characteristics has always largely shaped and will continue to shape America's way with the world. They are, in combination, what makes us American. Consequently, in my last chapter, I feel compelled to predict the way in which our cultural type will fit in the early 21st century global community. Be constructively critical of, and enjoy what follows.

Suggested Readings

Almond, Gabriel & G. Bingham Powell, Jr., *Comparative Politics Today: A World View*, 6th ed., Harper Collins, 1996, pp. 36-50 ("Political Culture & Political Socialization").

Art, Robert & Seyom Brown, *U.S. Foreign Policy: The Search for a New Role*, Macmillan Publishing Co., 1993, pp. 89-122 (America's three security eras).

Reich, Robert, *The Work of Nations*, Vintage Books, 1992.

Tocqueville, Alexis de in Richard Rapson's (ed.) *Individualism and Conformity in the American Character*, D.C. Heath & Co., 1967, pp. 1-14 ("Democracy and Individualism").

Chapter II

A Doctrine of Self Interest

Casting the Mold

In 1833, deTocqueville wrote "Democracy in America." No succeeding commentary has upstaged that insightful description of the American character, nor has any successfully discounted the essay's biting analysis. For over a century and a half, we have taken both pride and chagrin in the Frenchman's definition of our uniqueness—denying not even his charac-terization of our unfettered self-interest. We justify the trait as necessary in an environment of intense interpersonal competition. That condition both necessitates and legitimates the usually denigrated characteristic. Tocqueville exposed American society as a national experiment in admit-ting, condoning and using for the community's betterment this primal egocentrism.

Tocqueville's American was and remains a product of Western civilization's 18th century social Enlightenment and industrial revolution. We formed colonial and early American society on Immanuel Kant's self-centered challenge that we "dare to know," on Voltair's worldly view of human obligation, on Rousseau's mechanistic justification for social interaction and with a near fanatical devotion to John Locke's belief in the value and primacy of the individual. We erected the American state as England and Holland were building their global industrial empires. Manufacturing and trade for profit—those were and remain with us a state's best leverage internationally and its ultimate value. Tocqueville considered us blessed by being an integral and accepted part of Europe's advanced material supremacy, while being a virgin part not having to unlearn the habits and vested interests of its feudal relationships and pre industrial economies. We created ourselves without obligation to a lineage of self limiting societal obligations.

The framers of our Constitution were disciples of the Enlightenment and industrial revolution. None of the Philadelphia convention's fifty five delegates held lofty, aristocratic titles. Each, through self assurance, hard work, a pragmatic view on life and a willingness to compete had achieved material success. They were the elite of America's banking, investment, manufacturing, shipping, real estate, agribusiness and intellectual communities. Each respected personally earned authority and considered the individual accumulation of available wealth to be both an appropriate measure of worth and a right to be claimed. Commerce was their bonding.

With mutual respect, based on recognition that they shared a value structure, the Philadelphia delegates fashioned a process for indefinite cooperation—protections against both "unfair" personal actions and those of external authority. Our Constitution was a set of rules designed to entice collective activity by regenerating its product back into equitable individual betterment. Our Founding Fathers left Philadelphia hopeful that they had harnessed domestic public authority, while assuring its vitality by routing its profitable outcomes back into benefit to the citizenry. The agreed upon relationship undergirding that document challenged the accepted 18th century formula for community. It reversed an established relationship by mandating the supremacy of the individual citizen's wants over those of the community to which that citizen swore allegiance—a painfully honest statement of human aspirations, and a very dubious experiment from the perspective of social stability.

Our Constitution made government's attention to private interests compulsory. The most representative and citizen accountable branch— the legislature—was granted autonomous power in governance. Congress received sixteen enumerated areas of exclusive authority, six of them regulating the domestic economy specifically and the remaining ten designed to magnify Congressional authority over national economic regulation. A seventeenth power gave it the authority "to make all laws which shall be necessary and proper for the carrying into execution the foregoing [sixteen] powers. . . .", an umbrella insurance against unforeseen future challenges to legislative authority. To then shackle this preeminent branch to the individual private citizen, origination of all fiscal legislation— the lifeblood of a government—became the Constitutional monopoly of the lower legislative chamber, whose members had to reseek office every twenty four months. American private interests have always kept our government on a short leash.

Our regime founders established a nationwide free trade zone through creation of a single currency, prohibition of taxes on interstate commerce, but encouragement of import duties to block foreign made competitive goods. They centralized the reigns of public governance by making federal law the supreme law of the nation.

A federal judiciary, autonomous from and equal in authority to the legislative and executive branches, was invested as the austere guardian of individual rights, receiving grievances directly from citizens, and passing judgment on the admissibility of public authority's acts. Throughout the 19th century, our federal court's agenda supported individual freedom in pursuit of financial profit. More recently, it championed individual freedoms of speech, assembly and religious choice, and then defense of our civil liberties [protection against government encroachment] and civil rights [minority rights protection against the will of the private majority]. Through preference, habit and custom the American has nurtured litigation as a paramount means of insuring minimum governmental or societal constraint on individual liberty. Tocqueville foretold the future role of law and its executors when he commented, "Scarcely any political question arises in the United States that is not resolved, sooner or later, into a judicial question."[1] Today, in an atmosphere encouraging social conformity, litigation has become a much used tool both by those of us who struggle for autonomy and those who crave "political correctness."

By comparing the intended purpose of America's fundamental law to those of cultures assumed close to our own, our atypical insistence on individual freedom from societal constraint stands out. The constitutions of our two closest economic partners, Germany and Japan, were created in the late 1940s as recipes in domestic "political engineering."[2] Germany's early 20th century domestic instability resulted largely from that electorate's tendency to champion fascist and left radical agendas—two very collectivist but incompatible belief systems. Russell Dalton has characterized that state's "Basic Law" as a tool designed largely to prevent domestic ideological polarization. Unlike the American Constitution, it addresses the structure of political parties, and inclines the current society toward partisan and ideological moderation. Japan's constitution, developed and mandated by the 1940s American occupation authority, instills pluralism in a society which was weaned on authoritarian principles.

In Japan, postwar law making was shifted from the executive to the national legislative branch. Both constitutions mandate regime support for respect and defense of individual rights, but the German people, and the Japanese to an even greater degree, remain instinctively more appreciative of the need for collective activity than do we Americans.

Both the British and French heritages more parallel our attachment to individual dignity. French culture is infused with a love of individualism. The cry of "liberty, equality, fraternity" relates emotionally to an American's defense of "life, liberty and the pursuit of happiness." Yet, the French love of **fraternity**, and Jean Jacque Rousseau's proclamation of a necessary "social contract", reflect clearly our divergence. The French acknowledge a need for civilized man to as much be a social animal as an individualistic one. Created in 1958, their constitution concentrated authority in the national Presidency—a plebiscite. The recurring French rewrite of constitutional foundations reflects clearly that society's ongoing indecisiveness as to whether they want to be governed by an executive plebiscite or a parliamentary democracy. Yet, they never have championed the American belief that a national union could survive through the singular purpose of maximizing individual preferences and priorities.

British society, the often labeled taproot of the American political culture, never placed individualism in priority over community responsibility. Because British politics—the current Northern Irish issue excepted—has reflected centuries of comparative consensus and cooperative development, that nation never sensed need for one written constitution. An honored national heritage and deep respect for the major statutes and customs supporting that heritage, have been the only guidelines necessary to keep the British regime structure legitimate. British laws and customs support as much the exercise of collective responsibility as they do the defense of individual liberty. The British have always regarded American society as borderline anarchic.

Going Global

Individualism's credible promise of personal payback for personal effort has contributed substantially to making America the late 20th century's sole superpower. Admission that individuals strive hardest and most imaginatively when seeking selfish, not community goals has fueled the dynamism that marks both our creativity and work ethic, and the bonding which keeps us together as a nation. Globally, our "spirit" took off in the very late 1800s with Ransom Olds' and Henry Ford's founding of an automotive industry. Through parts standardization and assembly line manufacturing, the "tin lizzy" became an attainable possession of every thrifty blue collar American. Ford's roadster was available at $260.00 a copy in 1925, and his factories were producing a new buggy every 10 seconds. Four years later, America had 26,000,000 registered motor vehicles—one for every 4.9 citizens.

Widespread automotive ownership fueled the growth of allied industries—steel and oil. Regions of Texas, Oklahoma and California reeked of crude, and in 1870—by establishing the Standard Oil Company of Ohio, J.D. Rockefeller supported further expansion of Henry Ford's automotive empire. By 1877, Rockefeller interests refined and distributed 95% of American crude—such business concentration assuring a cheap and superior fuel. Andrew Carnegie's Bessemer steel works further stimulated our consumer culture, and by 1900 it was adding $40,000,000.00 in profits annually to his and his partners' personal holdings. Vast wealth, conspicuously used by the most productive few, and satisficing material comfort and convenience for all the rest; this became the acceptable reward broadly justifying American individualism. If Henry Ford and Andrew Carnegie can make it, so can I, and even if I don't, in this world my lifestyle is the best available. Private enterprise, mostly supported and infrequently regulated by law, legitimated our devotion to materialistic individualism. The pro management outcomes of the 1886 Haymarket riot, the 1894 Pullman strike and the early 20th century Dearborne demonstrations against Ford indicate clearly our willingness to limit government's responsibility toward labor to that of assuring equality of **opportunity** only, and in a context of stark competitiveness. We had come to accept an environment in which, for the sake of delivering the best product, losers lose massively.

After half a century of domestic growth, America's dynamic experiment in "collective self interest" felt ready for global application. By supplying the victors of two world wars with the accouterments and weapons of war, we had inflated our heavy manufacturing and transport sectors and whetted America's managerial skills toward worldwide responsibilities. At the same time, those wars trashed the economies of our wartime enemies and weakened those of our allies. Past allies and foes alike welcomed infusion from our healthy, expanded economy, and we spread our individualistic, capitalistic ideals as a by-product. The framework for America's late 20th century relations with most of the world was codified at Bretton Woods, New Hampshire in 1944. Open trade across state borders, easy and stable convertibility of all currencies, an interstate competitive impetus to enliven national economies and an American role within this network which broadly resembled—on a world spanning scope—the non interfering, supportive domestic role filled by Republican administrations from U.S. Grant through Herbert Hoover. In the 1700s, we Americans made a revolution to keep our profits at home. From that beginning, we experienced a natural and easy mutation to a society in which the pubic regime has one guiding mandate: To enhance fair **opportunity** for attainment of personal, material reward.

Are We Being Served?

Thomas Dye and Harmon Ziegler, prolific publicists on American politics, have concisely described the triangular relationship which constitutes politics in my country. Organized interest groups, Congressional subcommittees and executive branch agencies control our national public and private agendas. Through interest groups we largely germinate, shape and push the wants of our kaleidoscope of private wishes. Interests provide electoral funding, campaign support and practitioner expertise to needy legislators and executive branch bureaucrats. The legislators frame and sponsor bills which reinforce the goals of aligned interests and agencies. They provide the triangular relationship's statutory framework. The agencies, in executing legislative mandates, mold those loosely structured statutes to the wishes of supportive interests and Congressional committees.[3]

This triangular dynamic, while marginalizing our two-party structure as a policy player and erecting an institutionalized barrier to Presidential policy leadership, does provide a magnificent guarantee for attentive citizen meaningful influence in shaping public policy. Through early socialization, America's youths are taught the techniques and value of joint action. Clubs, associations, societies form and disband as involved citizens husband like minded associates to achieve common goals for individual satisfaction.

The prodigious collection of "cause" focused office suites surrounding our national and every state capitol are proof of the structure's pervasive presence and service to the ideal of "representative government." National (or Arizona) Association of . . . , National (or Alabama) Society for . . . , the staff expertise of those interests uniformly applies a non partisan, mostly ideologically centrist set of rules in competitive engagement. In one legislative year, initial focus is on aligned lawmakers, as the session frames its agenda. By mid year, both winners and losers shift their attention and assets to the executive branch agencies which carry out the lawmakers' mandates—either to intensify or soften the blow of the new statutes' intents. Toward the year's end, a third target arises as repetitive losers attempt court action to blunt damage to their quests. Then, as a new session begins, the lobbying community's attention cycles back to legislative allies. Fresh legislation can either reinforce or modify existing policy.

The process wonderfully services our competitive self interests. In societies in which the party structure creates and implements policy [parliamentary forms of governance] there is need for three, four or more major parties, for within each there must be membership awareness and then consensus on the entire current legislative agenda. In contrast, on any issue of perceived importance, we Americans will not commit to recognizing options or modifications, as we prefer not to defer to our fellow citizens on even lightly held positions. Detailed policy consideration and accommodation we leave to the British, German, Danish, Japanese, Australian and Singaporean people. In erecting provisions for a North American Free Trade Agreement (NAFTA), a fight between the leadership of the National Association of Manufacturers and of the United Auto Workers shapes the outcome. In our delicate Middle East balancer role, maneuvering between the leaders of the American-Israeli Public Affairs Committee (AIPAC) and of the National Council on U.S.-Arab Relations governs policy. American foreign policy could not achieve the fine tuning and flexibility [changeability?] it reflects if consensus based party input moderated its outcomes. We Americans prefer short-term, absolute and somewhat erratic outcomes to the moderated policy profile of party governed societies.

In our heritage diverse society, each of us feels entitled to be meaningfully heard, with our personal wants gaining sincere consideration by those who we elect to lead us. The interest group network is an imperfect structure in delivering those expectations, but we cannot come up with a more responsive substitute. Americans grudgingly accept the central role of money—campaign financing—in electoral success. Yes, we debate the smuttiness of marginally legal and absolutely unethical fund raising techniques, but invariably and consistently rise to the defense of any American's right to use personal assets for personal goals. Our law makers are considered executors or mid-stream links only, components in a looped system whose function is to turn private assets into legislation benefiting the asset giver. "Statesmanship" is, to the American, an occasional by-product which needs no special weaning. As long as the system validly and reliably provides the **opportunity** for each of us to become an asset giver—and concomitant benefit recipient—it is functioning effectively and fairly. For every asset backed interest, there will be a coequally backed competing interest. "Let the best group win, even if the victory is transient."

The Shadow We Cast

Collective self interest and free market economics are and always have been at the heart of American foreign policy. Until very recently, we voiced dismay at the Japanese Liberal Democratic Party's aversion to public influence sharing. Currently, we register disdain over China's denial of "human rights" to its citizens. Yet, close examination will disclose that America's concern over a partisan power monopoly in Japan and denied human rights in China are substantially cosmetic attitudes. Our real irritation is that their business practices seem harmful to American interests. Import-export trade barriers and financial and investment structural relations constitute our real beef with the Japanese. Import law fraud, the use of no wage prison labor for cheap manufacture and failure to protect American intellectual property rights are our irritation with Beijing. If those business practices are adjusted to our satisfaction, one party government in Japan and human rights violations in China will vanish as lead issues in American policy making. America's choice of "friends" has been and fundamentally remains based on our judgment of their worth as bilateral partners for American free enterprise activity.

Occasionally, our policy does stray from the cultural beacon of material self interest, but the irrelevance or declared detriment of this "misguided" focus quickly readjusts the agenda to a culturally compatible azimuth. For over a century, our interest in sub Saharan Africa was substantially to insure the uninterrupted and inexpensive flow of its resources to our or our chief trading partners' factories. We held little interest in Somalia until the late 1970s, when unfettered aid to an autocratic leader bought us use of Berbera's deep water port. That Indian Ocean location supported American "rapid deployment force" backup of our Middle East interests. The Somali society has never known conditions honoring individual self respect, and when the Bush administration endangered American troops—rightfully, our most cherished asset—

ostensibly to introduce democracy in that society, the American public was not supportive. In a December, 1992 poll, by a two to one margin, we registered preference for a limited U.S. role in Somalia—to deliver earmarked relief supplies only. In effect, if the Somalis cannot rid themselves of domestic savagery, it is none of our concern. If the material cost-benefit ratio in interstate relations proves negative, relations should be severed. In early 1994, the Clinton administration left the Somalis to their deteriorated fate, and that country's unimproved condition has disappeared from America's media and serious policy agendas.

If any state characteristic can be universally recognized as good or noble, probably America's image as the land in which all citizens receive essential dignity and equality before a common law is our best candidate for that distinction. Our schools teach entitlement of opportunity equality. Our many religious persuasions uphold the principle, and our courts interpret precedent and constrain public authority to honor it. Because Americans are bred to expect and insist on equal opportunity, United States citizenship remains the consummate goal of emigrants fleeing countries torn by authoritarian oppression. Asian, Latin American and African immigrants prefer access to America because it seems to promise two entwined opportunities, a heritage free chance to compete, and an environment in which successful competition can deliver personal riches. We apply that creed to all policy—foreign as well as domestic—then frequently find its extension in alien environments impossible to propagate. It did not spread in our 1960s Vietnamese policy, in 1970s Lebanon nor in Somalia in the early 1990s. Our intrusive attempts to replicate its growth may not take in Haiti and the former Yugoslavia, but if it does falter, remember the classic American response. We will withdraw undaunted as soon as the cost of implanting a more democratic society is thought to exceed the chance of our gaining our primary goal—benefit to America through the new relationship. Withdrawal cuts our resource losses and leaves our domestic well-being intact. Some non Americans understand our real priority, and our espousal of individual liberty and respect rings most credible to them if exemplified in our way of life, not as a sales package or export dictate.

Michael Manley, former Prime Minister of Jamaica, was an ardent advocate of the American domestic public-private relationship. He remarked often on our civic ability to bestow barely sufficient authority in government to make it a reliable block to private, monopolistic practices.[4] Through anti trust and tax laws, our regime has nurtured the growth of small, private enterprise. Personal opportunity and competitive growth were government protected conditions when President Taft fractured Standard Oil's monopoly in 1911, as it was when the Clinton administration confronted Microsoft's monopolistic bid with its browser forcibly implanted in the Company's popular Windows 95 program. In 1911, our federal government kept hopes alive among J. D. Rockefeller's business competitors, as it did in 1997 among Bill Gates' competitors.

Essentially, America's private and public institutions interact to deliver one cherished value, a sensible expectation that any one of us can succeed materially through effective competition. Private, free enterprise is the harshly competitive field of engagement and the source of reward for succeeding. Government is the referee, required to keep engagement fundamentally balanced between competing interests. Our way with the world was, is and will remain a projection of that established domestic condition. Occasionally, we will push its adoption by foreign societies. Consistently, we will compete to shape international relations which service its enrichment at home. Tenaciously, we will oppose any perceived foreign or domestic threat to its continuance and stability within the United States.

While most aware foreigners regard the consequences of our self-centered materialism with some condescension, sometimes with chagrin and anxiety, few consider adoption of this trait as healthy for their own well being or beneficial in meeting today's global dangers. They indicate, and we most frequently admit, that the trait results in money being our dominant commodity of reward. In America, comparative wealth goes further toward bestowing esteem, prestige and respect than does any other attribute—benevolence, intelligence, integrity included. It follows that we apply the financial inducement liberally to entice the best from our leaders. We pay them inordinately well. An evident outcome of that one-dimensional reward structure is the salary range enjoyed by our most successful corporate executives, and its contingent danger is manifest when seizing the salary becomes the sole goal of potentially productive and personally ambitious professionals and executives. They myopically game play the corporate or bureaucratic promotion ladder, striving for an improved product or service only if the improvement contributes toward their promotion potential. Paul Kennedy has defined one pervasive, damaging result of this reward structure on the contemporary American workplace. Our national economy can stay competitively resilient only if most of our slowly expanding workforce stays contributory to America's productive output—if we experience meaningful job expansion. One major consequence of alternatively substituting technology for employed workers, of not effectively retraining to keep them in the workforce, is to expand our welfare dependent sector—a deficit condition to any state's economy.[5] Yet, today's senior managers will not retain their well salaried positions—much less compete successfully to become corporate CEOs— by committing to effective workforce retraining as they introduce replacement technology. It is too long-range, too low profile in immediate results and requires much coordination between private and across public-private sectors. Technology's expansion means workforce "downsizing." The combination provides a short-term, high profile rise in productivity, with the initiators individually positioned to be considered for that prized CEO slot—with a one year salary reward sufficient to retire comfortably for life.

The "me first" focus is increasingly infecting management of institutions which deliver public or collective goods—products or services which are essential to a competitive economy but are seldom of themselves profit making if delivered with quality. Higher education is a clear example. Without a competitively educated workforce, across the sciences and arts, the dollar cannot compete successfully against the Yen, the Pound Sterling or the Deutsche Mark. Yet, chief executives in America's universities are increasingly adopting the corporate management style. Downsizing of professional and administrative staffs to achieve immediate operating budget improvements gains the short term plaudits of governing boards and, in recognition, a high end six figure salary for the "cost cutting" president or chancellor. Unfortunately, increasing class size, reduced funding of academic enrichment activities and increasing administrative error because of staff workload overload are by-products. They do not produce that more educated (competitive) graduate.

Consider the fit of the American way to the needs of a different culture. If we encourage the Russian society's emulation of the American— individualistic Lochean—drive for individual enrichment, we encourage that state's power elite to commit to a very destabilizing set of values. Within America, selfish motivation did and does contribute enormously to our overall national well being. This is substantially because a citizen legitimated public authority did and does shepherd our private endeavors, deterring those initiatives which seem potentially destructive of the domestic environment. But, in a nation in which government does not enjoy the publicly legitimated authority to police private competition effectively, to entice social development through satisfaction of individual betterment invites disaster. The currently influential Russians can best serve themselves by engaging their lucrative domestic "black market"— perhaps ultimately dealing in that state's most marketable commodity, enormous inventories of mass destruction weaponry. Put simply, those initiatives or motivations which have been and remain essential to America's prosperity will not produce the same results in societies with different values and modifying institutional networks. Oh, America seldom refuses an invitation to participate. We will be there, encouraging initiative based on self betterment, but common sense suggests wariness over the new environment's ability to take the transplant.

In effect, the core consideration is the fit between an appealing and contagious national environment which has come to terms with individualism's resiliency, and a world beset with dangers which are best addressed by interstate cooperation as opposed to competition. Retarding mass migration, environmental degradation and the proliferation of mass destruction weaponry come to mind. How well does American individual competitiveness fit in a world in which essential resource scarcity is a rising danger? We enjoy the world's highest energy consumption per capita, yet our oil based sources are foreign and limited. We import and consume more aluminum, copper, lead and mercury than any other industrial society. Our labor and management sectors, our rust belt and high technology industrial communities, our consumers and producers, our rail and roadway transporters cannot alter individual and sector incentives for a more collective national policy approach toward resource usage. Can we effectively lead a global effort toward the same necessary goal?

Uniqueness and the Fit to Needs

Less than two decades ago, we Americans reluctantly united in countering the physical threat posed by Soviet policy. That threat's eclipse has denied us the glue of national cohesion. America's foreign policy approach now reflects contradictory opinions on preferences and priorities, a lack of clear understanding about the nature of regional or global dangers and considerable domestic frustration at the unresponsiveness of our federal government in delivering decisive policy.

Why are we divided on policy preferences and priorities? Consider the divisive nature of America's acknowledged dangers. While public awareness of those dangers has increased over the past few decades, the nature of those challenges has shattered our consensus on how they should be addressed. We understand the absolute interdependence of our economy with all other major ones. Yet, that interdependence of manufacturing, marketing and financial processes has created new divisions in our once united domestic workforce. With money now globally mobile but labor still fixed in place, there are opposing needs between the blue collar and lower level white collar laborers of Indianapolis or Detroit and our corporate managers and stock holders seeking cheaper labor. Robert Reich, a recent Secretary of Labor, credibly worries that America is dividing into two adversarial camps, a secure, well educated and affluent minority whose worth is their cognitive ability to address problems effectively and a substantial majority whose physical skills no longer lead to employment. We can be proud that sixty percent of our public has become meaningfully involved in the foreign policy process, but relying on policy consensus from a public which is deeply divided between an advantaged minority of "symbolic analysts" and a vocationally warehoused majority will not deliver coherent policy. Will domestic division stall out America's global lead and responsiveness?

Why don't we clearly understand the dangers we acknowledge to exist? Consider the means by which we approach that agenda. Satellite relay, FAX, fiber optic transmission and the World Wide Web each overloads our sensitivity toward dangers. But each informative channel only describes the issue. The machinery doesn't think, offering objective analysis or solutions, nor does it place reported dangers in priority. In fact, each transmission treats its particular message as having preeminent importance. Environmental degradation, resource exhaustion, the spread of highly infectious or incurable and lethal diseases, mass cross-border population migrations, the proliferation of mass destruction weapons arsenals among feuding ethnic and religious factions, each danger seems to menace my country's well-being. Yet, no one danger cries out to all challenged communities as being the paramount one—as did the threat posed by Soviet military deployments. Consequently, which should we commit resources to first, second, etc., and can we be stirred to spend resources at all if that multitude of coequal dangers poses no **imminent** lethality to our comforts? Will we Americans, with public involvement uniquely necessary to foreign policy activity, ever be moved to reach a complex consensus in this chaotic but non dramatic environment of dangers—not threats? Without one omnipresent, unifying enemy, it is easier for 270 million individual interests to sustain an indifference, minimal understanding and ultimate stalemate in our way with the world.

Why are we so disappointed in the performance of our foreign policy leadership? Consider the mismatch between the operating structure of America's foreign policy bureaucracy and the demands placed by external dangers on that structure. Congress has unavoidable authority in shaping foreign policy. It constitutionally controls the process's funding, approval or rejection of all major policy initiatives and the monitoring of policy execution to insure program compliance with expressed public wishes. At the same time, Congress's 535 coequally influential members must each represent his or her constituents—a micro segment of the nation. Therefore, the potential for deadlock in policy funding, sanctioning and monitoring is high. Until about three decades ago, some foreign policy coherence existed because Congress granted our Presidents considerable autonomy and then support in conducting America's way with the world. At that time, Congress viewed domestic activity as distinct from and more personally [electorally] rewarding than its involvement in foreign policy. But, protracted conflict in Vietnam—without goal but with great drain on American lives and material resources—ended Congress's trust of autonomous executive branch foreign policy making at the very time when foreign and domestic policy were fusing in content. Congress became more involved. Can coherent policy result if that coherence is dependent on an institution which is intentionally and by member need responsive to the individual agendas of disparate and egocentrically socialized citizens?

Not only do we fashion foreign policy through an activist Congress which is suspicious of Presidential leadership, but both branches of our federal government have developed internal bureaucratic substructures which are, in turn, responsive primarily to competing private sector interests. Within Congress, traditionally foreign policy related law making committees seldom work cooperatively with committees which deal in traditionally domestic issues. In like manner, merger of policy development and execution between the executive branch's Departments of Commerce and Defense has not occurred as rapidly as has the issue content of our economic and our physical security needs. Will this publicly accountable but near discordant bureaucratic mosaic be able to conduct coherent and effective policy in today's world?

Finally, on a larger scale, America's way with the world may increasingly become one extreme [marginalized] approach through our tenacious defense of liberties and material wants. While most Western populations quietly envy and admire our love of self, and many materially destitute people flee their homelands in quest of American affluence and personal dignity, most of the world's people do not understand our individualistic style at all. Their cultures were not exposed to influences of the Renaissance, the Reformation, the Enlightenment nor to the personal rewards available during an unhindered national industrial takeoff. While we Americans carry the Western world's banner for individualism, it remains an odd belief system at best, a societally destructive one for those who are weaned on Buddhism, Confucianism, Islam, Taoism, etc.— most of the world's people. Samuel Huntington may be right. As our way with the world leads somewhat compatible Judeo-Christian societies in quest of more than our share of scarce resources and security, international relations may increasingly become a lineup of *the West against the rest*,[6] with America way out in the vanguard of the smaller team— and all because we deify individual freedom and an unobstructed opportunity to personally, materially succeed.

Suggested Reading

Huntington, Samuel, *The Clash of Civilizations and the Remaking of World Order*, Simon & Schuster, 1996.

Chapter III

A Present Centered People

There's Only Today

The phrase might be misunderstood. It needs definition by example. In the 1830s, our present centered nature both intrigued and confused de Tocqueville. He was puzzled by how a culturally diverse people could be so collectively happy while remaining "rootless, without memory or routines and having no common character."[1] And today, the image remains. Ann Davis, in comparing the influence of national cultural forms, concluded that approaches "encouraged an American concentration on the present and future and a Canadian interest in the past."[2] We are also quite insensitive to variations in national culture, and become confused when interpersonal relations go awry because our insensitivity plays out as a lack of discretion. Others marvel at our seeming "openness" while feeling private amusement at what they regard as our lack of cultivation.

Yet, cultivation requires respect for and action taken due to heritage— a uniquely weak perspective of the present centered American. Consider this. The predisposition to be guided more by expediency than by heritage was the means by which we rather rapidly consolidated a continental sized country of diverse, immigrant cultures. If not in the first generation, by their children's maturation the new Irish-Americans, Italian-Americans, Polish-Americans and now Asiatic and Hispanic-Americans uniformly became and now become "Americans." A short list of norms suffice in a society whose principal values have remained material well-being and the maximum possible individual autonomy in striving for that affluence.

Just as a simple, present centered set of norms gave us the physical mobility to create a 4,000 mile wide manufacturing and market network, that simple and direct credo expanded the network to a global industrial one and capitalized those ventures successfully. Business was and remains America's heritage, and—as markets and products are naturally in flux— business is a present centered pursuit. And yes, our "present centered" nature massively impacts the thrust of our foreign policy.—our way with the world.

My country was founded on a negative value agenda. The colonial settlers left Europe essentially because they perceived religious persecution or social ostracism and sought escape from those conditions, or because their positions in European society offered no reasonable chance of economic and social betterment. Our Revolutionary leaders' charisma was based on negative relationships with the British crown, and once America gained independence, there was little interest in readopting the political or social institutions which we'd just rejected by revolution. Those Americans rather courageously intended to build their society around a few simple and politically untested principles. Nor did the founders of contemporary America accept much of value in the lifestyle and institutions of native Americans. Ramsay Cook, in comparing us with the European founders of modern Canada labeled the United States "a society that had negated history and looked to the future."[3]

This future oriented characteristic massively differentiates us from our comparison group. British society is the model of sequentially stable maturation. British change invariably builds on British hereditary experience. The modern and prosperous French, German and Japanese societies, although they outlived a completely feudal past, have retained supports from those traditional pasts. Although the French love of liberty repeatedly inclines them to experiment with parliamentary democracy, as frequently, the innate inefficiency of democratic regimes pulls their preference back toward a plebiscite—a centralized, executive led regime which is comfortable because the certainty and grandeur of the Bourbon kings and Napoleon Bonaparte remain legitimate models today. In like manner, the German and Japanese societies take pride in the power and prosperity which the centralized control of Prussian and Meiji authority gave them. Only the American reliably wants a weak public authority because only the American believes that self governance is both a viable social alternative and a fundamental birthright.

This outlook's impact, on non Americans, has been and remains enormous. From a distance, the existence and allure of a place in which the governors are expected to serve the governed, and in which conventional expectation is for personal initiative toward self betterment, has substantially destabilized authoritarian regimes. Populations who felt oppressed and could emigrate, fled to America. We lured and then offered a safe haven to many western and central European sub cultures subordinated by 19th century industrialization and again to opponents of fascist regimes of 1930s Europe. Today, America's image appeals to Latin American subcultures disadvantaged by the rigidly class structured societies of their native countries. And, we have not been humble over this partially valid image. From the inscription on Lady Liberty's pedestal to the consciously weak enforcement of illegal entry across our southern border, Americans loudly maintain a seditious posture against regime types which conflict with the American perceived ideal.

Our founding and still governing Constitution reeks of a commercial, present centered outlook. From its 1789 ratification onward, we declared deviation from our European progenitors by fusing the responsibilities of executive head of government and symbolic head of state. We have never recognized a contradiction in the roles of a figurehead representing America's nobility and a politician having often to ruthlessly insure policy success. Our President is our chief mechanic, and what works currently must be both noble and best. We insured the President's sense of urgency by prescribing four year terms in office—one year to learn the job, two to fix problems or fuel policy successes and one final year to reseek office. The parliamentary technique of retaining a productive head of government for as long as his or her performance is publicly approved remains anathema in a nation which considers concentrated public authority an evil unto itself. In carrying the "virtue" of change to an extreme, we now mandate a change of Presidents after two terms.

In like manner, members of Congress operate on a short leash. House members, who monopolize authority to initiate fiscal legislation, must reestablish their job tenure every twenty four months. And term limits for both House and Senate members remains a viable consideration on our political agenda—the prospect of a limitation on performance for **all** elected policy makers. We are uniquely suspicious of any person with authority over us, and opposed to tenure with authority.

Yet, our near worship of change is a characteristic compatible with the inevitability of global socio-economic change. The policy profile of

America's post World War II administrations—each laboring under the two term limitation—has balanced competing demands of the Cold War and decolonization challenges rather well. The East-West (Cold War) focus of the Truman, Eisenhower, Nixon and Reagan terms successfully shifted to a North-South axis (decolonization issues) under Kennedy, Johnson and Carter. In Congress, 1970s generational turnover in the House and Senate was enormous but stably effected, and with it came wholly new executive-legislative branch relationships on foreign policy making and execution. A tradition freed, younger Congress reclaimed previous dormant Constitutional authority, and so cut down an increasingly "imperial" presidency.

Our Constitution was ratified with an intent to guard against frivolous change—thereby insuring against amending the basic law to irrelevance. Yet, twenty six concrete changes have kept its guidance current. Eighteen of those twenty six amendments, about seventy percent, were ratified in bunches within an aggregated time block of just twenty three years, in clusters accounting for only eleven percent of our lifespan as a nation. Those changes were mutations required to keep our maturing country socio-economically stable—legitimate. The first cluster, ratified in 1791, assured an individualistic electorate of the contractual availability of personal freedoms. The ten article Bill of Rights assured limits in the authority of our national governance structure. Amendments 13, 14 and 15 were ratified in the six years immediately following our Civil War. They legally ended slavery, the institution which had become our most socially damaging anachronism. Amendments 16, 17 and 19 became law at the apex of our industrial revolution, shifting some political and economic power from America's great entrepreneur families to the American laborer. The 16th, a graduated income tax structure, blunted the Morgans, Rockefellers, Carnegies and other industrialists from establishing perpetual family dynasties. The 17th and 19th amendments shifted political power to dispossessed citizen segments, the 17th through direct citizen election of U.S. Senators—rather than choice by elitist State legislatures—and the 19th through the franchise grant to the American woman. And, more recent reemergence of a sense of political inequity between citizen groups generated two more amendments. With the 24th, citizen minorities eliminated the poll tax as a bar to voting and the 26th gave Americans old enough to fight our wars voting power over those who decided when the wars would be fought.

Rootless Navigation

Consistently, commercial pragmatism for personal betterment has been our pattern of development. For one century, domestic challenges and opportunities kept us at home. There was potentially productive territory to be occupied and used, and the native American society requiring relocation. There were two increasingly incompatible economic structures—a budding industrial community and a slave based agrarian one. Civil war was the necessary solution. There was a continental sized industrial state to build. The private competitive incentive of hard driven businessmen consolidated our commercial framework. Rockefeller oil and Carnegie steel provided the material core. Leland Stanford, Collis Huntington, James J. Hilland and Cornelius Vanderbilt moulded a continental sized common market. A Wall Street syndicate, coordinated by J.P.Morgan's banking acumen, financed the process, and a nearly unbroken string of big business friendly Republican administrations fueled America's three decades of post-Civil War industrial growth. We were then ready for global involvement, not driven by a direct desire for influence, but through the more incremental, present centered need to control access to resources and markets worldwide, to be assuredly rich here and now.

Industrial growth necessitated immigrants—assimilated Americans—for a workforce. In the initial post-Civil War decades, resocialization was easy as Western Europe lost its industrious but socially disadvantaged substrata. In the late 1800s, southern and eastern Europe supplied an increasing share of new Americans. From 1871-1900, in excess of 8.4 million immigrants became American citizens. There was a bit of political context in their reasons for relocating and their expectations—some ill defined expansion of individual freedom—but they came primarily because they anticipated an opportunity to personally profit as part of a dynamically expanding economy. Therefore, they entered America with goals which were in harmony with the two established tenets of our present centered nature: personal prosperity through personal effort and the right to direct influence on a public environment which supported private, material betterment. They settled in Cleveland, Chicago and New York, bartering away the customs and outlooks of their European upbringing for American material prosperity. With their growing numbers as leverage, those late 1800s immigrants reinforced our present centered disposition through their pursuit of the good life.

With this self made, continental sized commercial state and culturally heterogeneous, personally aspiring workforce a late 1800s reality, America was ready for a global horizon. The inflammatory journalism of Joseph Pullitzer and W.R. Hurst gave cause to our expanding vision, and we focused wherever imperial weakness could least challenge American interests. The ossifying Spanish empire thus lost its Caribbean and Pacific basin holdings to our commercial encroachment. There was ample, untapped opportunity in both divided Manchu China and throughout Latin America for the spread of America's commercial reach. Any detailed American history text will reflect the commercially practical scenario used by my country in its pre World War I global "coming out." Our wartime and interwar foreign policy pattern remained consistent. "Just follow the dollar." Commercial interests delayed, for three years, America's entry as a combatant in the European land war, induced our troop commitment in 1917, and with defeat of the Triple Alliance, then returned our locus of interest from war fighting to domestic prosperity. Congress blocked America's membership in the League of Nations, and American diplomatic recognition of the newly established Soviet regime. Both policies occurred primarily because we lacked interest in relationships which promised scant immediate opportunity for commercial growth.

In his book *The American Pageant*, Thomas Bailey labeled this early and mid 1920s period a time of "cultural materialism."[4] Attentive Americans preferred minimum political ties to foreign regimes because remote control of essential contacts was considered sufficient linkage to fertilize domestic business opportunity. Acceptable trade understandings with French and mainly British governments, which held Trusteeship control of Middle East oil sources, assured America's need for cheap and reliable fuel. Strategic industries—mainly rail and shipping—were rapidly reprivatized for profit usage, and we drastically reduced our military inventories, not because of disgust over the horrors of the 1st World War, but because we had better things to do with our surplus income than buy peacetime warships and tanks. While Japan, Germany and Italy expanded their peacetime forces, our money went into a bull investment market protected by an increasingly impenetrable tariff barrier erected against competitive foreign imports. The commitment to business was not just activity of a small elite of wealthy and professional stock owners, but a sizeable percentage of America's comfortable blue collar and lower middle class white collar workers who made stock speculation for supplemental income their primary hobby. Our public's interest in the world centered on fueling immediate, material well being, supported by governmental oversight when personally of benefit but totally privatized otherwise.

When the United States entered World War II, there remained about twenty five years before our way with the world would again require retooling. The American public and leadership, our private and public sectors, younger and older generations uniformly regarded the early 1940s regimes of Hitler, Tojo and Mousselini to be a direct and immediate threat to our values. Our prosperity and leverage to maintain it depended on a peaceful and prosperous community of independent European states. It depended on assured, easy and cheap access to Mid East oil, mineral resources in Asia and accessible markets worldwide. The Axis powers threatened to permanently deny us those conditions, so America's industrial capacity, for a second time, backboned an international coalition which preferred global warfare to policy dictated from a fascist alternative.

Superiority in resources, numbers of troops, materiel and ultimately technology won us World War II. Victory also exhausted the international reach and domestic prosperity of all wartime allies except the Soviet Union. In less than five postwar years, we Americans came to sense as much threat from that sole competitor—Joe Stalin's regime—as we had held against the wartime fascist coalition. By 1950, Eastern Europe was consolidated under direct Kremlin control, and most West Europeans feared the growth of Soviet influence across their continent. That condition again threatened our vital trade relationship with Europe. The Kremlin then openly announced and demonstrated an intent to support revolutionary movements worldwide. By 1950, a Communist regime controlled mainland China, converting the world's most populous state to a seeming political ally of the Kremlin. China had been a major American market, and it would continue to exert influence throughout East Asia. Our and our West European colleagues' entire East Asia market and source of resources was threatened.

Ideologically, America's Cold War period response was inconsistent. We subverted or walled up the leftist regimes of Salvador Allende and Fidel Castro, while supporting the Marxist regime of Joseph Tito. We allied with the rightist dictatorships of Salazar, Franco and Marcos, while bankrolling United Nations military action against the rightist dictator of the Congo's breakaway Katanga province. Yet, the pattern was extremely consistent toward the singular policy goal of defeating mainly Soviet global expansion. Whether a state's regime was Marxist or fascist was of little consequence if it reflected hostility to Moscow's or Beijing's influence, or if American action could woo it away from Soviet or Chinese influence. Ours was a logical agenda for a strong nation convinced of threat to its prosperity and unhindered by political ideology in forming its agenda. Our pragmatic counter contained no loyalty to past obligation. We reestablished the economic health of our wartime enemies before the surrender documents' ink had dried. Germany and Italy must be strong in facing Moscow in Europe, and an equally stable Japan was nourished to counter Asian expansionist moves of both the Soviets and Mao's China.

The agenda worked for us until the mid to late 1960s. By then at least four factors enticed reevaluation of the singular Containment goal, another shift in focus to maintain our treasured wealth and personal liberty. First, twenty years of confrontation had consolidated the Soviet and American spheres of influence. The Cold War had incorporated all states, and both Moscow and Washington temporarily acknowledged the other's turf. Kremlin policy consequently became less overtly threatening—more bureaucratically irritating. Second, our postwar renovation of the German and Japanese fascist regimes and economies was so successful that two stable democracies began challenging American global economic hegemony. If their comparative growth continued, we would soon share prosperity, partly on their terms. Third, nearly three decades of confronting foreign based threat had been met by postponing domestic needs. Those needs began straining our stability. A declining purchase power for most Americans, socio-economic degradation for minorities which erupted in urban warfare, and widespread recognition that the federal executive branch needed taming. Americans felt a need to accent domestic priorities. Fourth, this present centered people had led a global military crusade for nearly three decades, and we were increasingly bored with the scenario. It was time to end the Cold War friction.

Not all attentive Americans preferred a major policy shift. Habit, comfort with established attitudes and often personal vested interests in the Cold War bureaucratic structure kept many citizens "hard liners" or "hawks." Consequently, domestic consensus in our outlook on the world ended. Another twenty years would elapse before the division would begin to heal. Not since the late 1800s, when America went international, had such an overhaul of foreign policy outlook and practice been required. But we mutated successfully in the late 1890s from a purely domestic economy to a global economic power, as we had thirty years before that from an agricultural exporter dependent on slavery as an institution to a non slave based industrial power. Just as the 1850s Pierce and Buchanan administrations faced the challenges of going industrial, and the later Cleveland and Harrison White Houses dealt with instabilities of going global, Ford, Carter and Reagan each tried to reconcile the conflicting agendas of hawks who lobbied for continued Soviet-American military confrontation and doves who favored attention on challenges to the global trade network brought on by the instabilities of colonialism's end.

The last gasp of Soviet imperial pretensions prolonged the validity of the "hawks'" agenda in America. Through their Afghan invasion, targeting of West European capitols with SS-20 medium range missiles and development of a global naval presence, the late Brezhnev, Andropov and Chernenko regimes kept the East-West face off alive. Then, Mikhail Gorbachev's team changed permanently the face of Soviet foreign policy through its unilateral global disengagement and ultimate imperial disintegration. Georgi Arbatov, the Soviet "Americanist" and close advisor to a string of First Secretaries, was half right in predicting that the Soviet Union's end would disorganize America by denying us a unifying enemy.[5]

What Arbatov did not understand is just how transient—present centered—my countrymen are in outlook. Because we have real interest only in what needs doing to currently service our prosperity, each generation uses a clean slate, redefining what seems most challenging to those material values at the time. Because policy influence comes from multiple domestic communities, any one committed sector can generate massive pressure for change.

For example, America rapidly altered its global outlook in the late 1980s, with the Reagan administration's monetary policy reversal. During the "Gipper's" first term, White House economic planners had maintained the previous decade's strong dollar policy, partly to pay for high priced imported oil and partly to attract foreign investment capital to the American economy. Then, in Ronald Reagan's second term, American trade, investment and banking interests unilaterally created a weaker dollar to spur American exports worldwide. With Congressional support, they also structured a policy reversal in our three decade long economic relationship with Japan. With the Soviet threat gone from Asia, a more competitive Japanese-American manufacturing and trade relationship advantaged us, so we began chipping at that Asian ally's favored but no longer essential bilateral position.

George Bush codified the new American approach to an old friend, implementing the Structural Impediments Initiative and Super 301, two policies designed to more equalize our relationship. Like Buchanan's or Cleveland's before him, his four years in the White House were a watershed administration, with our public's demand for massive change in policy priorities propelling our policy makers. President Bush enjoyed an 88% public approval rating in March of 1991, and his subsequent conduct of the war to extract Iraqi forces from Kuwait was pervasively considered masterful. Yet, his approval rating had fallen to less than 40% by late 1992. The media, the Congress and the public considered a half century of Cold War concerns over guns (force) as passe. As third party Presidential aspirant Ross Perot identified, America's first priority interest had returned to the domestic economy—to butter first (wealth).

The Clinton administration initially acknowledged that priority. In socializing experiences and global outlook, it does constitute a new generation's acceptance of power. The Clinton White House can not complete America's policy transition in eight short years. A complex and globally entangled state of over a quarter billion vested interests takes longer than eight years to set on a new course. Yet, process and policy are now seeded to meet three new challenges. First, until very recently, Americans dealt with domestic and foreign concerns separately. Over the past two decades, the fusion of those issue areas has become increasingly obvious, and long established processes for handling each separately are under serious revision. Second, the process of assembly line manufacturing, which gave America its late 19th and early 20th century prosperity, can no longer support that relatively high affluence. The American work force is painfully realizing the need to change its way of earning a living. Third, three centuries of high intensity, total force, interstate war between advanced nations is winding down. The unstoppable proliferation of horribly destructive conventional weaponry is one core reason why advanced states can no longer fight each other profitably. America, as the globe's sole military superpower, recognizes the need to refit its instruments of coercion in order to address the type conflict which it can fight well and with rational purpose—low intensity shows of force, material support to some allies and those mid intensity engagements recently termed "peacemaking" and "peacekeeping" operations. The 21st century global environment will sprout more than the three challenges, and we Americans have both a cultural asset and a deficit in meeting the needs of change. The asset is our present centered nature. It eliminates both nostalgia and habit as impediments to change. We will naturally seek new tools to meet new needs. The equally influential deficit to our fashioning workable options will be addressed in Chapter 6.

A Floating Anchorage

As one considers the American value structure, a flexible—transient, if you will—foreign policy agenda is the only one which fits. Our attentive public must believe that it can, whenever it wishes, meaningfully impact public policy content. Our governance system's legitimacy is based on that belief . Yet, that same public's active involvement in such "grand activity" will, of necessity, be sporadic and lightly informed. Earning a personal living and daily family activity necessarily take precedent. Most citizens undertake national policy involvement only as a "feel good" hobby or when its content seems to impact jobs or family. The end result, for those few whose daily job is managing our foreign policy, is that public influence on the direction of America's way with the world seldom provides unified guidance—and when it does, that direction is only as to the broad "what" is to be done, not the more precise and difficult "how."

Because America was founded on the principle of meaningful, responsible public control of public policy, a uniquely authoritative or powerful role is given to the American media. It alone can provide the geometrically increasing volume of information necessary for true public awareness about our increasingly complex international environment. Satellite relay, fiber optic transmission, a bonding of the public to television and now information collection using the world-wide-web are necessary links in keeping our governance system working and legitimate.

Align America's foreign policy processes with the following model. From George Washington's to Bill Clinton's administration, there have been four sequential steps used in policy creation and execution. An agenda is somewhat agreed upon domestically, modified through negotiation—peacefully or with force—between us and involved foreign interests, ratified domestically as acceptable in its modified form, and then implemented. The American attentive public has always influenced directly the first and third steps, agenda setting and policy ratification. Those two steps address the "what", not the "how", and they require only some situational knowledge and consciousness of preferred goals to perform well. The media supplies the necessary background knowledge, and both they and elected leaders suggest goal formats constantly. Policy negotiation and implementation, in contrast, are full time and complex vocational undertakings, requiring detailed knowledge of the issue under consideration. Those two steps are done by our foreign policy professionals, with the President at their apex.

Because of our present centered perspective, our President's job, compared to those of a British Prime Minister or French President, both provides more creative opportunity and is more difficult to undertake. In the heritage rich British and French societies, perspective on events and opportunities incorporates a historic dimension—an expectation that applied policy be in tune with the customary or culturally appropriate British or French way of acting. This always present boundary partially limits options available to the two heads of government, whereas the American President can consider and expect public support for almost any avenue which he projects as appropriate to the current situation. Yet, the domestic latitude available in shaping American policy comes with a price. First, because heritage generated considerations are weaker in America, our President faces a wider diversity in domestic policy options—and consequent public preferences-than do his British and French counterparts. He must expend more energy and creativity in coalescing public opinion to policy support consensus. Second, once a policy is launched, the American public's appraisal of its worth will rest more on the more unpredictable demonstration of success in meeting goals, less on the more grounded criterion of meeting long established norms. To a far greater extent, his score card depends on showing constant movement and winning.

I'll conclude this picture of my people's extreme present-centered nature by describing the extent to which the comparison set of major, affluent societies—the British, French, Germans and Japanese—reference their pasts in conducting their ways with the world. You should keep in mind the four step policy process and the triangular influence structure—private interests, Congressional committees and Executive branch agencies—described previously and central to American governance. National differences in respect for use of the past as a guide for the future, will be obvious.

The British are enamored with their past, and their governing regime's policies incorporate preservation of a heritage based "style." Their hereditary Monarchy, largely unencumbered by the transient demands of an electoral constituency, is the most identifiable guardian of that style. Through public statements, diplomatic innuendos, weekly private conversations with the Prime Minister and a very visible presence within the realm, the Monarch subtly but daily influences the course of British foreign policy. Elisabeth has been the British Queen since we installed the Truman administration. That condition alone constitutes comparatively great continuity for British policy. British parliamentary structures and processes as well incorporate consideration of their honored past. While our bicameral Congress represents both population density (in the House) and an equal voice for each state (in the Senate)—but in a totally contemporary venue—the British bicameral structure divides along an entirely different dimension. The United Kingdom's upper chamber, the House of Lords, is composed mostly of members whose posting is granted by birthright. Most of the remaining thirty percent are "life peers", members whose personal contributions have ennobled the realm. The Lords' collective prime role is to guard the context of Commons generated legislation against sharp divergence from long established British values. Stable democracies erect their bicameral legislatures to address the fault line which most concerns them—the Americans to represent the diverse and present centered interests of fifty different sized states, the British to mold contemporary policy activity generated in the Commons within limits prescribed by their heredity based self image.

As with his American counterpart, the French President is both head of state and of government. But with that condition, the similarities mostly end. Since Charles deGaulle established the 5th Republic, the French presidency has been a national plebiscite—a constitutionally centralized executive leadership structure which appeals to the French people not only because its concentrated authority develops policy movement, but also because its grandeur and style equate to the eminence of 18th and 19th century France. The Elise Palace's senior resident has far more policy authority than has the law approving French legislature and law interpreting court system. He marginally doles executive power to a Premier, whom he appoints, but holds foreign and defense policy direction monopolistically as "reserved powers." He sets the legislative agenda and substantially controls its climate through his authority to dissolve France's lower chamber—the Assembly—and because of the prescribed short sessions during which that body is in session. Both the French and American Presidencies constitute the only direct electoral mandate from their entire electorates, but the French President wins a seven year term and can be reinstated for as long as that electorate holds trust in its executive leader. In crisis, the President has "emergency powers," substantially creating a temporary near absolute monarchy. In contrast, America's regime structure requires the constant and coordinated use of **shared** powers between three separate branches, each applying its view of how best to address the situation at hand. We believe that pragmatic, detailed, interbranch bargaining on a policy's content generates good governance. The French much more rely on symbolism, precedent, tradition and the grand view of one publicly chosen leader. While American policy seeks to fix problems incrementally and through compromise between affected parties, the French offer "leadership" based on an image of national cultural cohesiveness and respect for a much honored past.

Today's Germans most resemble Americans in projecting a present-centered outlook. Yet, Germany's current cultural mix is too new and possibly too externally established to be assuredly lasting. For the past fifty years, a genuine shame and rejection of their 1900-1945 foreign policy record has haunted successive German generations. From the late 1940s through the mid 1960s, all Germans vociferously absorbed guilt, and in Western Germany, where the American presence heavily impacted the Federal Republic's population, Germans largely adopted the omnipresent American way to substitute for a way of life gone bad. Yet, over the past few decades, generational replacement has increasingly distanced younger Germans from handed down guilt, and native cultural characteristics are reemerging. The Germans' love of their past will always be less extensive than will be the heritage based pride of Germany's neighbors. Germany was not a unified country until the 1870s, and it has its early 20th century relationships to outlive. Additionally, the experiences of building their state more resembled United States experiences than those of Great Britain, France or Japan. Prussian authority focused on what worked materially, with policy success measured along physical rather than spiritual or more philosophic lines. To that extent, the German will always hold more the American present centered focus in forming policy than do the other three nationalities, but the Germans' increasing reacceptance of and reference to their own short heritage makes their perspective far from a clone of the near totally present centered American outlook. Consider this. Since the end of World War II, my national electorate has burned out nine Presidencies—Bill Clinton's being the tenth. Over the same time frame, France has changed Presidents four times and Germany five. Helmut Kohl led Germany while America changed from Reagan's to Bush's and then to Clinton's leadership. In considering that three state comparison alone, which of the nationalities seems most prone to employ contemporary micro-adjustment as a governance end in itself?

Although Japanese Prime Ministers come and go with frequency, that regime adheres to and respects its heritage perhaps most of the four comparison nationalities. Until August, 1993, Japan's postwar regime belonged to one party alone—the Liberal Democrats (LDP). Prime Ministerial changes reflected only substitution of one of a half dozen LDP factions for another—a perpetual game of musical chairs by long term associates within a tightly knit ruling group. That elite, in turn, derived from the pre World War II Japanese establishment, whose progenitors were the late 19th century Meiji Genro, whose forefathers were the Tokugawa Shogunate of the early and mid 1600s. Japanese society, from the reign of Emperor Jimmu in 660 AD, has been centralized and responsive to one hereditary elite community. Respect for social order has always been, and remains today, a stronger value than individual self concern. Harmony and mutual support between institutions remains a Japanese hallmark, with the pervasive Shinto belief system fusing both public and private, religious and secular endeavor. They term the process of national leadership selection "amakudari." It starts with an intensive education of the most competitive youth sector, preferably ending at either Tokyo or Kyoto university, followed by about twenty five years of service in and out of a national ministry and corporate enterprise. Because positions as senior ministers are few, those most competitively productive Japanese not selected to run ministries—the most preferred capstone positions— receive near equal authority as senior members of a Diet LDP faction or as chief executives in a Zaibatsu (one of the business conglomerates which now exercise multinational corporate influence and enjoy its status). The clearly delineated Japanese culture constitutes an established, long transmitted guide to Tokyo's way with the world. Before they are seriously adopted in Japan, contemporary values are fashioned to conform with a centuries old outlook.

Yes, the identifier "a present-centered people" fits us Americans uniquely. Victory over any personal challenge, winning in sporting competition, scientific breakthrough to overcome a disease, personal wealth achieved from a birth in poverty, each is a uniquely honored accomplishment within my society, and each is best realized by focusing on today's assets and conditions, not yesterday's.

Chapter IV

The Myth of Isolationism

A Misleading Definition

Too frequently, the American character is attributed with a deep preference for isolation from international involvement. The image is of a people who reluctantly engage other societies only to save some universal good from extinction, compete justifiably for our share of material well being or defend our state against sensed physical aggression. The scenario is that, once we've regained the moral high ground, insured our prosperity or neutralized the threat, we return invariably to our preferred concern—that of nurturing America's domestic environment. Noted analysts of our character have only recently modified that isolationist bent a bit, acknowledging our reluctant acceptance of very long term global involvement. Allegedly, our trade and monetary structure have ensnared us in a global network, and our worldwide military presence is required for the stability of that network. We don't like the new conditions, but accept them as necessary.

The champions of this standard profile often cite the Monroe Doctrine as proof of our isolationist preference, and reference the domestic focus of the following seven decades as further evidence—with the decade of the Spanish American War, America's Boxer Rebellion involvement and the Philippine Insurrection being a brief abnormality. Allegedly, America again withdrew early in the 20th century. We delayed entry into World War I, left Europe precipitously after victory and opted not to join the League of Nations or diplomatically engage the new Soviet regime. Our sequestering supposedly encouraged the 1930s German and Japanese regimes' aggression against their neighbors. America was then forced into World War II, and our postwar global engagement has remained contrary to our collective preference.

The foregoing, widely held view would make us fundamentally isolationist, if it were true. If it validly reflected both our actions and their underlying motives, we would bear an intrinsic dislike of engaging foreign communities. We would acknowledge the existence of very different value sets internationally, and be quite content if our moral outlook remained the choice of Americans alone. If it were a true character reading, we would have been considerably less engaged than we have been over international crises of the past half century. We would most often have opted for a **secondary** curative role or none at all, trading a slight erosion of our global prestige or paramount affluence in order to keep "separation from foreign messes." But, in Chapters 5 and 6, we will explore two major American characteristics which are incompatible with an isolationist outlook. A people cannot be ecumenical—believe that they have an inherent right to trade and establish their interests everywhere—and be isolationist. One also cannot believe that a common set of moral principles apply globally and be isolationist. At this point, let it suffice that I illustrate how we have come to so widely misinterpret "unilateralism" as being "isolationism."

American's have never been isolationist. We have frequently registered little interest in foreign involvement which promised us little reward, more interest in using available assets domestically because the expected reward seemed greater by applying the assets at home. But a nationality which acts independent of others and mainly on its own behalf is being a solo player or unilateralist—not an isolationist.

Proof Through Actions

Perhaps by examining directly the policy content of our 1823 Monroe Doctrine, both the distinction between being an international isolationist and a unilateralist and the condition that we are decidedly the latter will be illustrated clearly. Consider five state or regional players of the 1820s environment: the United States, Spain, Latin America as a region, Russia and Great Britain. The Spanish were the core colonizers of Latin America, but by the early 1820s their hold on that region was eroding. Domestic and European continental challenges posed more immediate concern in Madrid. A growing sense of autonomy, within the Caribbean and South

American colonies, accompanied that loosening of Transatlantic ties. Simon Bolivar and Jose de San Martin gave voice to South American wishes for autonomy, and Brazil achieved independence from Portugal fourteen months prior to President Monroe's famous Congressional report. This independence movement was a natural aftershock of two popularly based uprisings, the American and French revolutions of 1776-81 and 1789.

Ironically, when Monroe prepared and delivered his address, he was probably thinking more of Russia and American control on our northwest border than of Spain and conditions to our southeast. Russia claimed America's Pacific coast as far south as present day British Columbia, and had established trading posts in San Francisco Bay. Monroe was merely codifying the indirectly stated expectations of Washington, Hamilton and Jefferson that America's contiguous expansion was not to be impeded by foreign regimes. This claim encompassed a zone around continental North America sufficient to assure "breathing space"—ultimately the western hemisphere.

Russia clearly understood Monroe's warning. She backtracked through present day Canada, establishing her jurisdiction at the 54°40' latitude in 1824—at the southern tip of present day Alaska. Russia was removed to the frigid northwest tip of North America and the dynamic, young United States regime had sent a clear diplomatic statement to all long-term European colonizers. At some future time we would increase our interest in other European holdings, expecting them to accommodate. More immediately, we had a nation-state to consolidate. Then, we would probably have a hemisphere to harmonize, and both should remain our exclusive and rightful pursuits.

President Monroe probably secondarily considered London's somewhat latent interest in Latin America. Consistently, imperially inclined Britain had shown interest in the continental sized holdings of other, weakening colonizers, and the British were a bit unsettled by the energy radiating from the "American experiment". Yet, Latin America was not their priority concern. More accessible and lucrative colonial expansion was available in Asia and Africa. In August, 1823, British Foreign Secretary George Canning requested that we develop a joint statement of interest in Latin America. The suggestion was a low budget ploy, possibly tossing some easy earned benefit to British interests. Under the advice of Secretary John Quincy Adams, President Monroe delayed a direct response. His December Congressionally routed statement—the Doctrine—

was intended to make our position unmistakably clear. The areas surrounding the United States were to be free of any foreign influence conflictual with America's interests.

When examined in the context of interstate interests of the time, the Monroe Doctrine in no way reflected America's desire to isolate our polity from foreign contact. It did signal that we expected potential foreign competitors to stand aside as we drew on domestic and proximate foreign assets in nurturing our growing nation. It reflected a preference to "go it alone".

Both geography and 19th century interstate relations largely kept America on a unilateralist tack. Unlike the Germans, who always faced all neighbors across close and easily crossed borders, the Atlantic and Pacific oceans offered natural barriers to encroachment from all potential great power rivals of that period. To our north and south, contiguous states were too small to seriously counter United States policy. Unlike the British nation, whose comparative wealth depended on globe-spanning control of resources and trade linkages, the United States inherited a continental sized country of fertile and resource rich land and a century in which to establish that grant unhindered. Both in natural conditions and the requirements for economic consolidation and political maturation, America was blessed. Those conditions and requirements fostered our unilateralist stance in foreign policy.

Moreover, for nearly two centuries, we succeeded eminently in whatever goals we erected. America developed the world's largest economy and its strongest military presence, and we became a symbol of opportunity for individual material prosperity. With such credits, could a belief in the attainability of autarchy be far behind? We developed a preference for fashioning foreign policy with no"entangling alliances." Joint, collective, coordinated, mutual, shared interstate policy has come to connote ineffective, near fruitless, feckless, weak, indecisive policy solely because it is shared policy. We are sold on doing things, as Frank Sinatra so concisely put it, "my way," and this attitude and behavior pattern have both been centuries in the making and habit forming in their outcome. In effect, the agenda of unilaterally constricted American policy now begets a continuation of unilateral behavior as a function of consistency, habit, the defense of vested domestic interests and bureaucratic continuity.

By the time we decided to join the imperialists' club, "singularity" was widely recognized as an American foreign policy style. Within half a decade, my country established its rather permanent presence in the Caribbean and Pacific basins and in East Asia. Our war with Spain to secure Cuba, Puerto Rico, the Hawaiian Islands, Guam and the Philippines; our pressure on China, France, England, Japan and Russia to assure American trade leverage in the Far East; and our "strong arm" against Colombia and diplomacy with England to build and control a canal across the Isthmus of Panama were each solo American ventures.

Just prior to the Spanish-American war, we had a $50 million investment stake and a $100 million trade stake in Cuba. Native insurrection was rising, and the island's Spanish authority was harsh in its counter revolutionary measures. The Hearst and Pulitzer newspapers laid a jingoist base for American intervention—ostensibly to relieve the Cuban population of oppression, mainly to secure American interests in Cuba. The February, 1898 scuttling of the battleship Maine in Havana harbor—conveniently attributed to Spanish sabotage—provided the excuse for invasion. "Remember the Maine. To hell with Spain," and President McKinley was steamrollered into war. Assistant Navy Secretary Teddy Roosevelt used the opportunity by dispatching Commodore Perry's Pacific fleet to seize Spain's Pacific holdings—Guam Island and the Philippines—and the Hawaiian chain was annexed in July. By August, American troops had decimated Spain's Philippine based land and naval forces, and emplaced Emilio Aguinaldo—a compliant Filipino revolutionary exiled in Asia—as head of the archipelago's government. By August, the poorly equipped and supplied Spanish garrison in Cuba had signed an armistice, and Puerto Rico also tumbled from Spanish control into America's grasp. Late that year, at the Pact of Paris, Spain ceded its Caribbean and Pacific basin holdings to my country for the face saving sum of $20 million.

Then America turned its attention on the mainland of south Asia. China's mid 1890s defeat in war with Japan had led to rampant foreign partitioning of the weakened Manchu dynasty's port cities. Russia, Germany and Japan joined already established Britain and France in erecting leaseholds and economic spheres of interest deep into China's sovereign territory. Responding to the encroachment, patriotic Chinese loyalists attacked European enclaves along China's coastline. American manufacturing and trade interests, fearing our lockout from mainland Asia, contributed 2,500 troops to the Boxer Rebellion's European relief force. As participants in the economic partition of China, we then had some right to shape imperial policy. Autonomously, America announced that China was to enjoy commercial and territorial integrity—a subtle shift in inter-colonizer relations which expanded United States penetration into British, French, Russian and Japanese holdings. We expected a "free market" atmosphere in the Orient—the Open Door policy.

One final solo move capped our global "coming out." A connector was needed between my country's Caribbean and Pacific holdings and interests. Only with that passage could trade flow safely and cheaply between the two basins. Previous understandings bound the United States to include Great Britain in any canal project across Central America. In 1901, American cajoling diplomacy assured us autonomy to both establish and fortify the connector. The ink was hardly dry on the Hay-Pauncefote Treaty before we energized Panamanian revolutionaries to rise up against their Colombian governors. Colombia, prepared for a native uprising, had stationed troops in close proximity to the hot spot. My government interposed United States naval forces between the revolutionaries and the Colombian troops, then de jure recognized the breakaway Panamanian insurgents as a state. American engineers, protected by American troops, then constructed the canal through a ten mile wide corridor administered jointly by Washington and the newborn Panamanian government. A wish of America's 19th century whalers, traders and missionaries had been consummated. In less that one decade of assertive foreign policy, the Caribbean and Pacific basins were linked and opened to American manufactures and trade. This is a strange legacy for an isolationist people, not so strange for one which is rather unilateralist at heart.

The expectation that we will most often act alone, and on a global stage, was validated worldwide in the early 20th century. As the great states of Europe went to war in 1914, America initially abstained. Our early neutrality is often mistakenly regarded as resulting from a preference for non involvement—for isolation from the perpetual conflicts between European states—much as was our 1918 precipitous withdrawal and refusal to take on League of Nations membership. Yet, for the first three years of World War I, the issue before the American public was infrequently whether we should absolutely abstain from fighting, but rather the basis which would justify our inevitable entry as a combatant. Teddy Roosevelt, standard bearer for the electorally defeated Republican party, wanted early American entry on the side of the British. He envisioned potentially grave damage to America's new global trading position and prestige if strengthening Germany was allowed to defeat the French and British field forces. Roosevelt wanted early American commitment sufficient to force the Kaiser's planners to negotiate for peace—a pragmatic power-balancer perspective on interstate relations.

Our ultimate rationale for entry became the standard credo applied in American foreign policy decision making from 1917 until today. "Wilsonianism" rejected America's use of force for such a utilitarian reason as providing an interstate power balance. Woodrow Wilson fueled our belief in "American exceptionalism." We must propagate individual freedom and prosperity globally. We must "make the world safe for democracy" by neutralizing the anti democratic spread of German influence. Notice that neither Roosevelt's nor Wilson's views made accommodation for an isolationist abstention. The former sought our entry early to achieve equilibrium in forces. The latter wanted self assertive entry later in defense of a self proclaimed set of principals, and to spread those principles as universal mandates. Neither basis fits "isolationist" principles. Both are expansionist and are user friendly for a unilateralist. Wilson's more principled option won. Freeing the world of political tyranny and preserving its economic accessibility provided the imperative justifying our war declarations of November 1917 and December, 1941. The imperative—autonomous defense of American prosperity and propagation of our universal moral code—has anchored our global involvement throughout the Cold War and beyond.

America has followed consistently the adage that states have temporary allies, no long-term friends. In late 1956, we acted alone against three unquestioned allies, supporting the Kremlin's wishes and the needs of Soviet aligned neutrals. The British, French and Israeli's had engaged President Nassar's Egyptian forces in order to secure the Suez Canal, an oil artery vital to our allies' economies, but in the hands of a regime more friendly to the Kremlin. Termed "Buccaneer", their attack caught both Washington and Moscow off guard. Understandably, the Soviet hierarchy reacted negatively, warning us that if America did not stop the invasion, Soviet entry might be necessary and could precipitate a superpower faceoff in the Sinai. A cluster of non Cold War aligned governments echoed the Soviet view that Buccaneer was wanton aggression, and my government used its dominant influence in the International Monetary Fund and World Bank to force Britain, then France and Israel to end their campaign. The binding ultimatum was our cloaked threat to break the Pound Sterling if Britain did not withdraw from certain success.

Less than four years after Buccaneer, we unequivocally demonstrated to the British that American interests came first in bilateral relations. Britain had been developing a rocket able to carry a nuclear warhead eastward across Europe. "Bluestreak", that rocket, experienced multiple developmental cost overruns, and was questionably able to penetrate Soviet defenses when it neared the prototype development stage. Early in the Eisenhower administration, we promised the British our "Skybolt" medium range rocket, and our close NATO ally placed reliance on that joint undertaking—an American developed rocket carrying a British developed warhead. Then the American administration changed, and President Kennedy's new Defense Secretary, Robert McNamara, undertook a review of costly Pentagon projects. The Skybolt seemed, to McNamara, not cost-benefit effective for the American inventory. Without Transatlantic coordination, he scrapped final development, leaving the British reduced means of delivering their warheads. From the late 1950s onward, most adult Britishers have regarded America's foreign policy approach as unilateralist—an image held by most of America's Cold War partners by the late 1980s.

Brief reference to a few additional American initiatives should validate our solo methodology. There was the Bretton Woods arrangement for global trade and monetary management, a joint creation of the major wartime allied governments. In 1944, cooperating states agreed to an economic network with the United States at its hub. With the strongest economy, we would control currency exchange rates with the dollar and gold latched as a fixed anchor. America would oversee postwar recovery and development through established, multinational institutions, and our comparatively prosperous economy would open its doors as a market for the goods of American approved foreign states seeking development. In return, we would gain influence over the participating states' foreign and domestic policies because such policy derived inherently from the American role. We would also gain the opportunity to expand America's manufacturing base into those state economies—through both stock (portfolio) and managerial (direct) investment. The process required cooperative commitment, and, over its twenty five year life span, became institutionalized throughout the non Communist world. For us, the hegemon, the problem was its progressive drain on American resources— the investor in weak ventures and an open domestic market for many. Precipitously, in 1971, the Nixon administration unilaterally ended the system by releasing the anchoring dollar to float against other currencies.

We instituted harsh controls on development loans and defended domestic manufactures with protective import tariffs. Our solo policy shift helped stall economic growth across East Asia and Western Europe and plunge less developed economies into chaos.

There were also the American leaderships' and publics' slow responses and unique evaluative criteria in discarding military confrontation with the Cold War's two Communist monoliths—the Soviet and Mainland Chinese regimes. The Beijing regime's 1971 acceptance into the United Nations General Assembly was against the strong and lone opposition of the United States. Throughout that decade, our major Cold War allies increasingly encouraged us to drop opposition to China's placement in a permanent Security Council seat, but official American policy remained steadfast in support of Taiwan as the Chinese nation's appropriate representative, and the American public majority endorsed that awkward line. Concurrently, American administrations conducted a decade long secretive, tension lessening, bilateral discussion with Beijing, suddenly reversing our official course by officially accepting the Peoples' Republic as a Security Council replacement for Taipai in 1979. We had autonomously determined that the Chinese Republic, acting as a colleague, would give us counterweight against the Soviet Brezhnev regime's late 1970s global influence expansion. In like manner, we reconciled Soviet-American Cold War hostility, not in the early 1970s, when Western Europe erected trade linkages with the East block and began serious peace overtures with Moscow, but nearly twenty years later, when American interests alone were best served by ending the superpower confrontation. Only when the Gorbachev regime renounced control over the Soviet sphere in Eastern Europe and alone withdrew its offensive military forces from that region did we join our NATO allies in accepting a Soviet regime as other than an implacable foe. By the very late 1980s, it was apparent that compatible manufacturing and trade linkages were forming across the Cold War European divide, and that further American hostility toward Moscow would translate into our being locked out of a coalescing Eurasian economic sphere.

Then, there have been our more recent, hemispheric relations. Throughout the 1980s and early 1990s, with public endorsement, American governments enforced American priorities on nearly all states of the Caribbean basin. Our myopic support of El Salvador's Duarte government against all alleged center and left leaning alternatives has caused us continuing embarrassment. The Duarte regime and that state's notorious "death squads" operated in parallel. Unconstitutionally, Ronald Reagan's administration supported the rebel faction of Nicaragua with weapons, supplies of war, clandestine training and encouragement against a government diplomatically recognized by most Latin American and West European governments. We openly blocked efforts by groups of Latin American states to reconcile the conflict between Nicaragua's Sandanista government and the American backed Contras, and when the Constitutional illegality of the American cabal was publicly disclosed, a considerable portion of the American public praised the cabal. Abraham Lowenthal, founding director of the InterAmerican Dialogue, summed up our blatant intrusion into Latin and South American regional relations when he wrote, "the 1989 U.S. invasion of Panama, the deployment in Latin America of U.S. military advisors in the anti-narcotics campaign, the extraterritorial enforcement of U.S. drug laws, and the recurrent neo-Wilsonian urge to export democracy—all suggest that the **unilateral** activist impulse of the United States has thus far survived the Cold War's demise. . . ."[1]

Half a world distant from the Caribbean, the Bush administration demonstrated how completely American unilateralism survived the Cold War's demise. America led the multinational coalition to oust Saddam Husein's forces from Kuwait. The American commitment to first block further aggression at the Saudi Arabian border, and then destroy Iraq's offensive forces was not contingent on any other state joining our little war to restore Western oil supples and Kuwait's sovereignty. Most major oil users did contribute—frequently after American rebuke—but pre deployment coordination was a secondary priority. The Desert Shield and Desert Storm campaigns were American conceived and attained American made goals—to include post conflict erection of a sanctuary for Iraq's Curds within Iraq's territorial borders. This last action appeared necessary to us alone. Curds are considered domestic terrorists by Saddam and by our Turkish and Russian Desert Shield/Desert Storm allies. Yet, America's "point man" role in the war and immediate postwar consolidation are considered, by most of the American public, to be the Bush administration's finest hour.

In like manner, the Bush administration's international trade and manufacturing policy was aimed almost exclusively at short-term enhancement of America's comparative advantage. In 1989, Congress and the White House, pressured by domestic business interests, introduced *Super 301*—a statutory mandate that the administration identify discriminatory trade practices by our partners and promise retaliatory action. Within its first year, the project took damaging United States action against the Japanese—its acknowledged prime target—Brazilian and Indian domestic economies. Michael Mastanduno, a Special Assistant in the 1989 Office of the U.S. Special Trade Representative, had this to say of "Super 301, "Virtually the entire international trading community objected to Super 301, perceiving it as **unilateral**, coercive, and contrary to the spirit of multilateral cooperation in the General Agreement on Tariffs and Trade"—a largely American erected and executed global policing activity.[2] Concurrent with Super 301, Congress introduced the invasive *Structural Impediments Initiative*. It required our government's economic planners to publicly identify and criticize domestic aspects of the Japanese society which hampered easy bilateral trade—how the Japanese used their land, how firms purchased materials, how Tokyo spent Japanese tax dollars and even how the work and recreational habits of the Japanese people insulated their society from foreign products. The Kaifu government was stunned by America's myopic insensitivity to alternative cultural patterns.

Again, our self serving agenda was apparent at the 1992 Rio Earth Summit Conference, the 1994 Cairo Conference on Population and Development and the 1995 Berlin Conference on Climate Change. By the time of the Rio Conference, the world's sole remaining superpower had a uniquely parsimonious lending policy for foreign state development and was frugal in its trade arrangements with the less developed community of states. The Japanese were most liberal in development aid. The West Europeans, under prior Lomé convention arrangements, had virtually eliminated import tariffs from established commodities on which African, Caribbean and Pacific (ACP) states depended for export earnings, and had stabilized the purchase price of those products. America went to Rio to maximally block other delegate states' forests from domestic development. Led by Malaysia, the Global South confronted the American delegation with the position that the natural assets of developing states were not America's to control. One year following the Rio meeting, over 150 states had signed a biodiversity convention, a profit sharing contractual accommodation between the Global South holders of resources and Global North producers of resultant finished goods. The United States singularly refused to be a participant. At the 1995 Berlin Conference, our delegation employed hair splitting legalese to excuse its failure to reduce industrial carbon emission.

The predilection for solo action reappeared when Presidential candidate Bob Dole championed unilateral American arming of Bosnian Muslims encircled in Serajevo and again when most elected American officials assured their voting constituents that they would strongly oppose American military personnel in the Balkans ever being placed under foreign commanders. Unilateralism is with us now through the Helms-Burton statute, requiring United States retaliation against any state trading with Castro's Cuba if the exchange involves present or prior nationalized American property. Few allies can understand our continuing overt hostility toward the Castro regime, what with the absolute collapse of the Kremlin's international challenge, much less our intent to punish friendly economies for trading with the Cuban people.

Why We Act, But Act Alone

Actually, the source of American unilateralism is not hard to determine. No other contemporary society has experienced the aggregated stimulation generated by the following five conditions. First, my country's founding elites perceived their regime creation to be a unique experiment. Second, we were advantaged in inheriting a continental sized land area, temperate in climate and rich in natural resources. Third, we enjoyed unusually secure borders during our domestic founding and consolidation. Fourth, by the beginning of the 20th century we had in place an industrial infrastructure which could supply adequately the material needs of a victorious coalition in global warfare. Fifth, we exited World War II as the only western nation whose domestic economy was not in ruins. We thus inherited a singular leadership role in physically securing and economically rehabilitating the non Communist community of states. Certainly, an inclination to think primarily in terms of one's own national wishes and conditions is the pervasive outlook within every state. What is unique to us Americans is the success which we've continually experienced in applying self centered policy criteria—our ability to, over two centuries, benefit from that egocentric reference point and consequently instill it as a credible guidepost to future outlooks and actions.

Every state experiences constantly changing relationships with others. Conversely the main characteristics of its peoples' culture change much more slowly, if at all. Over the last half century, the conditions which rewarded American unilateralism have changed. Seeming erosion of domestic harmony and in our ability to project force against foreign challengers have made us question our uniqueness. The advantages of a huge and cohesively developed land area set off from potential enemies geographically have eroded because of the increasing irrelevance of distance and the lethality of weapons technology advances. The economic advantage we gained from introducing and then embedding the assembly line industrial manufacturing system was diluted when war ravaged foreign economies leap-frogged with sophisticated service and high technology commodity industries, and reaped the profits inherent in trading forward edge products. Today, America senses its need for colleagues. Production assets of each advanced state are partly responsive to direct—not portfolio or stock—ownership by foreigners and capital control is multinational. Just as the chassis of an automobile—the largest single component—is unable to perform its primary function without support from such smaller components as the exhaust, electrical or fuel systems, America is no longer able to assure individual liberty and prosperity to our people without the willing cooperation of the European Union and Japan.

Yet, we remain unilateralist because deeply we are no longer American if we are not autonomous. Self defeating in a way, isn't it? Also laden with inconsistency between many promises made to our people and others and our actions. We do preach Adam Smith's doctrine of free market global trade, then expect others to subordinate their policies to our liking— which is John Maynard Keynes applied worldwide. This conflict does bode interstate friction over the next decade, and America's probable course through those shallows will be addressed in our final chapter.

Red Flags for America's Way

For now, consider the misfit between real global conditions and America's preference for autonomy in addressing the following three issues. First, consider our need to achieve economic and political incorporation of the past Soviet Union into the Western community. That region is too omnipresent, too globally important to be other than stably included. Yet, the very extent and nature of its need mandates a relief package much larger and more complex than the United States alone can deliver—many times larger and multifaceted than was the 1940s Marshall Plan for Western Europe. Also understand that we Americans are not the most appreciated or accepted source of relief in Russian or Ukranian eyes. The West Europeans—principally the Western Germans through their 1970s-1980s "Ostpolitik" and the diplomatic overtures of successive

French governments—sought Cold War reconciliation long before America discarded its image of an "evil empire." How well will unilateralist America work **in concert with** the European Union to support needs of the newly willing but cautious and misaligned states of the ex Soviet Union?

Second, consider that Germany and Japan probably still need a continuing American military presence responsive to perceived needs of their regions. Older generations in neighboring states remember the early and mid 20th century oppression they endured at the hands of expansionist German and Japanese regimes. Thus, an American military presence in East Asia and Central Europe does provide an external security assurance as the vibrant German and Japanese economies reinforce those states' regional preeminence. Yet, the German and Japanese nations should not, will not remain America's clients indefinitely on any major foreign policy dimension. Their economies must incorporate increasingly the manufacture and sale of components with defense related technology inherent to them—photonics, biotechnology, advanced communications systems, etc. Will America assume easily a less central role in Europe and East Asia, as generational replacement in Europe and Asia erodes fear of a strong Germany and Japan, and as those two states undertake expanded security roles natural to their commanding economies?

Third, consider alternatives to the unilateralist, hegemonic security posture and role which we demand in nuclear non proliferation and in keeping a near monopoly in strategic nuclear weapons. Can we expect other great societies to indefinitely refrain from developing a credible, domestically controlled nuclear deterrent? If not, wont proliferation be inevitable, and will unilateralist America then **amicably** surrender its sole remaining monopoly—that of global policeman?

Opportunities for us Americans to exhibit cross cultural magnanimity, or even understanding will soon be legion. But then, if we do exhibit such flexibility in relations, will we be acting like Americans? Cultural characteristics grow for fundamental reasons. They are resilient, sometimes of benefit in lubricating a nation's pursuit of its basic values, sometimes a retarder. Regardless, a nation is essentially stuck with the substance of the national personality—its cultural framework—and we Americans are only starting to appreciate the frustrations of a Gulliver who needs the support of smaller and very different Lilliputians.

Chapter V

We Ecumenical Americans

I Belong Here

The trait, by itself, defines only a level of individual or group awareness and appreciation of community involvement. Alone, it has no ethical content. The characteristic varies in intensity across cultures, some societies wanting more foreign contact than others.

Throughout the 19th century, the British were perhaps the world's most ecumenical people. British manufactures and trade, and those activities' attendant global security requirements, necessitated worldwide involvement. Then, Britain's early 20th century relative economic decline was accompanied by a souring of domestic interest in foreign involvement. Following World War II, British governments relinquished their Mid East and Asian involvement to American or energetic native interests, and the British people shifted focus to European regional concerns. Conversely, the Germans adopted a global presence only after that war. German leadership and the German people thought regionally before the postwar "economic miracle." The Federal Republic's recovery stimulated a global reach, and vibrant production for export has kept contemporary Germany engaged worldwide. The Spanish and Portuguese perspectives followed yet a third time table. Madrid and Lisbon's 16th century policy shapers were among the most ecumenical of late Renaissance societies. Their mercantile trade and conquest spread across the Mediterranean, Caribbean and Pacific basins. Spanish Catholic renditions of a universal moral code provided both the model for modern interstate mercantilism and initial rationales for contemporary international legal principles. Then, north European competition eclipsed Catholic Spain and Portugal's colonial status, and with that eclipse the interests of Iberia's population turned inward, eventually extoling the reverse virtues of economic and political autarchy during the Salazar and Franco dictatorships. With sensed opportunities inherent in post World War II West European economic recovery and integration, the Spanish and Portuguese perspectives have again changed. There is now a resurgence of interest in the European region and Latin America. "Hispanidad" has returned in a 20th century context.

Yet, uniquely, as the British have tethered their ecumenical outlook, the Germans have newly acquired a global perspective and the Spanish have a rediscovered interest in the wider world, America entered the community of nation-states with its agenda setting public sensing entitlement to and need for world involvement, and we have—for over two centuries—never altered that "wide screen" outlook. Yes, this trait is incompatible with the oft touted "American isolationism." But again, the isolationist label, if affixed to the American character, is a misnomer. Whenever America shunned interstate involvement, it was solely because, on a cost-benefit scale, domestic opportunities appeared more rewarding than foreign ones. Three factors largely trigger an American ecumenical inclination.

Foremost, we associate if the association generates personal benefit to us. The strong American drive for comparative individual well being includes the belief that material comfort requires exchange—interpersonal and interstate trade. Prosperity is a relative status. Therefore, to stay prosperous, we must continually fertilize economic intercourse. After gaining political autonomy through revolution, we formed a thirteen state union, not because the thirteen involved communities sensed much cultural affinity, but to achieve viability as a large commodity producing and trading unit. We wholeheartedly received and have never seriously questioned Adam Smith's "invisible hand" and David Ricardo's "competitive advantage" theories of an open global trading environment. Substantial basis for our entry into both 20th century world wars was to preserve a global, open trading environment for American use. We were "naturals" at shouldering economic hegemony of the 1950s and 1960s non Communist world. The Bretton Woods Agreement and its World Bank and International Monetary Fund instruments, the General Agreement on Tariffs and Trade and our many early postwar bilateral and multilateral trade agreements reflected America's ease with the global involvement which attends domestic affluence. My country's recent defense of Saudi and then restoration of Kuwaiti oil resources only continued the American theme. Foremost to us is the nurturing of material values. Accommodation across ethnic, religious and political divides therefore becomes a necessary and sensible intermediate step in goal attainment.

The second and third factors nurturing the American's global perspective are our somewhat unique geographic condition and our very unique moral outlook—this latter trait to be only identified now. It will be addressed in depth in my next chapter. America developed as a substantially unified country—the east with the west coast. Through New York, New Orleans and San Francisco, its interior was supplied, early on, employing an extensive railroad network. This network facilitated near uniform development across a 4,500 mile breadth. East and West coast Americans, therefore, look with equal interest and attention across the Atlantic and the Pacific. Much like the British, but with a more massive geographic core, we have developed the mentality of "islanders" sitting in **our** global sea. The ecumenical outlook is inbred.

Only on the moral dimension do the American and British world views diverge. Two centuries of unusually successful and essentially unchallenged domestic development have weaned our moral self assurance. We have come to believe the American way to be right—morally—*for the whole world*. British foreign involvement remained material, never aspiring to the role of global prophet.

One might better understand the context of America's ecumenical proclivity by viewing her economic outlook as mutating over three distinct development stages. From our Revolution to the American Civil War, America focused domestically. The framework for competitive expansion was laid over those seven decades. By reapplying profits from a near monopolistic control over the raising and sale of the world's best cotton fiber, we developed the world's most lucrative grain basin, erected a world spanning merchant marine fleet and experienced a wave of industrial inventiveness. A somewhat different outlook grabbed American interests from the 1870s through the mid 20th century—a geographically wider one. With acquired capacity to produce and sell, we became the world's model Westphalian state—economically top dog, militarily dauntless and assured that our relative material comfort and power required continued global involvement. The past half century, the third time period, is demanding a second readjustment in our attitude, not movement away from the need for engagement, but a growing awareness that there are intractable limits to how much we can control external forces. The neat Westphalian mosaic of discrete, big state players, each with its own client states and with the United States as the "chairman of the board" is coming undone. We increasingly employ a reactive more than a proactive agenda.

Fledgling America

My country's initial locus of interest was domestic not because we considered irrelevant or disliked relationships outside America's territory. Much as an ambitious youth dreams of an eminent adult future, we savored and considered inevitable the time when our activity would parallel that of the most affluent European states. Our early status—and resultant relative well being—were inward looking because the national conditions of strength were adolescent. Investment capital—domestic and foreign—was scarce. The American labor force was stable and most attune to agricultural employment—with the personal hardships of a British factory laborer's lot providing a distant reminder of the comparative virtues of a living earned off the land. Our transport network and organization to capitalize on domestic resource potential were underdeveloped. Because early Americans preferred rural life, a minority of us produced finished goods, and our largest foreign trade associate—the British—preferred keeping it that way. They effectively protected their manufacturing and marketing lead.

Yet, the base for a globally competitive garment industry was growing in New England. The cotton gin made processing of raw cotton commercially profitable. Roadway, canal and rail network expansion eased the movement of both raw products from the American South to New England and the distribution of finished garments to northern retail outlets. New England's snug ports and ample, navigable rivers became natural assets, and an influx of Irish immigrants—forced from their homeland by failed potato crops—provided cheap labor for the manufacture of cotton garments. Then, with Elias Howe's sewing machine, New England was ready to compete with the British garment industry, worldwide.

Well before our Civil War, the transport link for global trade was in place. American packet ships carried oriental tea and spices to British and continental European ports, and fast Yankee clipper ships raced the British merchant fleet for dominance of the sea lanes. By the mid 1840s, my country had extracted trade and tariff concessions from China equal to those of any trader. A decade later, Commodore Matthew Perry's warships forcibly opened Japan to American trade, and we had muscled near monopolistic control of the Hawaiian island chain. We had refitting stations for merchant ships and whalers and a start point for American missionaries determined to alter the ethics of the Pacific basin's populations.

Topographically, both distances and alignment of mountain ranges and riverbeds should have stimulated a predominance of the north-south over the east-west axis as America's population spread and culturally harmonized. Yet, the nation's 4,500 mile wide east-west axis increasingly served our drive for commercial enhancement. By our Civil War's eve, America had 30,000 miles of railroad track, mostly in the industrial north and cited westward. The discovery of California gold provided an ancillary impetus to westward expansion, both through the rail system and round the hemisphere shipping. Few hopefuls found gold in California's riverbeds, but unlucky transplants had alternative employment at hand— involvement in some aspect of our China trade. As Americans moved west and the Orient's products flowed east, our heartland developed complementary commodities, grain and livestock. Silas Cyrus McCormick's mower-reaper provided the mechanical edge to capitalize on a vast basin of near ideal soil and climate. The result was wheat and meat for the world at the very time when England's Corn Laws committed that country to dependency on foreign grown foods. Tea, spices, our share of the opiate trade, cotton, wheat, beef, whale by-products and the American missionary's crusading spirit—all delivered by a world class landmass and sea transport network. Hardly the stuff of an isolationist people.

Yet, this growth rested on profits from one product alone—short-staple American cotton. Britain was the world's leading cotton cloth manufacturer, with twenty percent of her workforce so employed. Eighty percent of that cloth originated in America's southeastern coastal bottomland. Cotton was pre Civil War America's one option for balanced trade, constituting 57 percent of the value of American exports in 1860. Cotton provided America with diplomatic leverage against the great regimes of Europe. But supply of an agricultural raw material would never, alone, advance America to the stable affluence level of the great manufacturing regimes. Commercial inventiveness, the production of diverse finished commodities for a world market, erection and maintenance of a transport system to support that global enterprise, this agenda dominated activity across the northern two thirds of my country in the mid 1800s. Add to this dynamism the zeal of American religious missionaries who accompanied our overseas, commercial expansion, myopically believing their message to be of untainted benefit for targeted recipients, and the overall profile is that of a people needing elbow room. ·

Numerous observers of British and American growth patterns have remarked on the peaceful, evolutionary way in which the former people shifted lifestyle patterns, and the violence which has most often accompanied American lifestyle change. There is no more dramatic example of that difference than the mid 19th century manner in which Britain first and then the United States went economically global. Recognizing the necessities and opportunities of commitment to a multi continental manufacturing and trade base, the British government passed the Corn Laws in mid century. Britain's farmers were thus made a substantially tertiary and unprotected appendage of the domestic economy. The farming family moved to Manchester or Coventry, becoming textile or iron foundry wage earners. In contrast, America's prime commodities shift required the four year slaughter of 600,000 citizens. Two increasingly antithetical socio-economic environments had developed domestically— 1789 to 1860. In the North, inventions were making the mass production of profitable commodities feasible, traders and whalers were profiling a bottomless market for those manufactures and our basic societal driving force, defined much later by Franklin Roosevelt as our *third great freedom*: "Freedom from Want," propelled the *Yankee* interest. The South's antebellum economic and social structures, which had been previously necessary and therefore deeply imbedded, had become a mainstream block to industrial growth. The South's antebellum economic and social structures were expunged through civil bloodshed.

A Global Grasp

Post Civil War industrial expansion necessitated both the steady introduction of management creativity and a much larger work force than we had in the 1870s. We rewarded successful entrepreneurs with huge personal wealth. We met the latter requirement through waves of emigration from Europe and Asia, with the new arrivals' infusion of cultural diversity further fueling our ecumenical outlook. We then negotiated or forced a global network of markets, and exposure of those Americans who secured and serviced those markets further whetted our worldwide involvement.

Technological application conveyed our industrial growth. The steam turbine stimulated mass production. With the Bessemer and Open Hearth processes, steel's per ton price was reduced from $300.00 to $35.00. The use of interchangeable parts multiplied the potential for volume production. Then, Henry Ford introduced the "family automobile" to both the American and European markets. Organizational genius—stimulated by an unleashed profit motive—drove Carnegie and Ford to manufacture, Vanderbilt to transport their raw materials and finished products, Rockefeller to harness needed energy sources and Morgan to bankroll the total enterprise. America was poised for global trade leadership. We needed only more workers and an expanded market.

Between 1870 and 1900, my country's population both doubled and urbanized. In 1860, less than 15% were urban. By 1920, over 42% called cities or large town environments "home." A substantial minority of both the city and farm dwellers had been born abroad. Between 1820 and 1900, 20 million people emigrated here, most early arrivals being easily absorbed because of their western European upbringings. The cultural backgrounds of post Civil War immigrants more challenged the Yankee/Anglo base model. They arrived on our eastern coast increasingly from southern and eastern Europe—over 50 million in the 1880s alone. On our west coast, Japanese-American and Chinese-American communities blossomed, the former as a spin off of burgeoning trade with Eastern Asia and the latter largely providing labor to expand our continental railroad network eastward. By 1880, San Francisco's population was nearly ten percent Oriental. The linguistic, religious and custom based potpourri resulting from this influx on both coasts kept America ecumenical.

And, in tandem, our quest for and defense of markets sustained worldwide immersion. By the very late 1800s, my country was using gunboat diplomacy repeatedly: against Canada and Britain to contest control of the Bearing Sea seal harvest, against Britain to establish influence in the Venezuela- British Guiana region, against Chile over naval transit rights at that country's ports and against Germany for basing rights on the Samoan Islands. Captain Alfred T. Mahan supplied the framework ideology, the view that America must be a first line global naval power. The Pulitzer and Hearst presses reinforced that mind set across our public, and the politics of Secretaries T. Roosevelt and Blaine and Senator Henry C. Lodge transformed the ideology and public mandate into policy. American reaction to the February, 1898 sinking of the battleship Maine in Havana Harbor was not the reaction of an indignant and isolationist people, reluctantly implanted on foreign territory and unjustly treated by foreign governments. When the Maine sank, America had a $50 million investment stake in Cuba and a trade stake of twice that value. The incident provided justification for war with Spain in the Caribbean and Pacific basins—for the formal erection of an American global imperial reach.

An Unsettling Third Stage

Within fifty years of America's global emergence, the basic international linkage that made the Westphalian system came apart, and Westphalia's successor was initially in harmony with the American "world outlook." Since the mid 1600s, advanced and wealthy states had politically and economically used client states as their industrial resource sources and as part of their finished products market. The control was bilateral and exclusive—one colonizer to its colonies—and was considered justified and appropriate by the colonizer and a goodly percentage of the colonized. In the late 1890s, we Americans entered this patron-client system with energy and a sense of entitlement, but late. We had to push the overseas Spanish authority aside, the Russian, British and German colonial interests a bit less. We had to accommodate to a junior partnership role in this 200 year old pattern. However, the drain of two world wars, the development of indigenous leadership in many colonies and a change in the type manufactures which delivered most profit—reducing the major states' need for traditional basic resources—made the Westphalian (colonial) structure increasingly unstable and unprofitable. The structure was, by the late 1940s, rearranged with a pattern more accommodating latecomer America's preferred way in doing global business and exercising control over its business network. High cost, low density and synthetically composed manufactures, intellectual and complex service industry refocused the interstate trade and manufacture pattern horizontally. We became the hub of a network wherein the economies of the advanced and rich states link with each other, the remaining two thirds of national communities being reduced to tertiary targets for resource and market enhancement. The contemporary American—post Westphalian— pattern for interstate relations honors state sovereignty in legality, then deploys manufacturing, trade and financial activity almost oblivious to those sovereign state boundaries.

Mid 20th century America introduced the Multinational Corporation. Initially as a means of circumventing another state's control over its domestic markets, then as a way of increasing short-term gains from the fluctuating cost of labor and the value of currencies, finally as a means of on-site tailoring of commodities to meet local tastes, we moved toward direct foreign investment in manufacturing processes and toward multi continent assembly of any one large commodity. With Truman Doctrine financial support to the eastern Mediterranean region, Marshall Plan reconstruction of western Europe and a lopsided but guaranteed bilateral trade relationship for the recovery of war prostrate Japan, we achieved global economic preeminence. Leadership in the multinational decision processes of the World Bank, International Monetary Fund, General Agreement on Tariffs and Trade and a host of Cold War inspired bi and multinational trade agreements has retained that position for America.

As with the cosmopolitan 19th century British, the 16th century Spanish and Portuguese and the Romans before them, Americans have traveled the world in uniform, principally to defend the foreign sources of our domestic affluence. Through NATO, CENTO, SEATO, the Australia-New Zealand-U.S. alliance and bilateral arrangements with Japan and Israel for four tense decades, we kept the Kremlin's hands off of what we considered our property. Today, with Russia's concession to our stronger global grasp, we are attempting a remake of our Cold War enemy's economy—an attempt at perpetual economic and attendant cultural expansion through reapplication of the dollar and American technology.

One consequence of this global remake is the manifest interdependence of all participating states' economies. Texas Instruments must warn Congress that any protective tariff against competitive Japanese imports will endanger our ability to monitor Japanese technology breakthroughs in the banned commodity sectors. America's business leaders and workforce warn European Union lawmakers that their reduction of Japanese auto imports will most adversely impact employment levels in Ohio, where the autos are assembled. Domestically, we adjust the economies between individual states to meet foreign interests. For example, United States policy commits us to assure the politically moderate Arab states' regimes that oil, their one lucrative export commodity, has a global market. Their pricing is manageable, their production costs are low and corporate America is heavily invested in the region's refining and storage processes. The stability of those moderate Arab regimes rests on possession of one industrially essential resource and, conversely their stability is our guarantee that the resource will remain cheap, readily available and somewhat secure. In consequence, American and Mid East economic and security interests largely determine the metropolitan economies of New Orleans, Louisiana and Fort Worth, Texas. An American who loses employment in Louisiana's declining oil industry had best move to Fort Worth and build Saudi Arabia's fighter bomber fleet. This type of trans state security-economy reciprocity is impossible to square with a predisposition toward isolationism. Ecumenical isolationism is a contradiction in more than terms.

Home Just Isn't The Same

In the mid 1940s, a war exhausted western community mandated that America assume hegemonic status. That mandate fit our ecumenical character. Now, just half a century later, those war wearied associates have recovered their ability and desire to exercise global influence. Yet, ecumenical America has not volunteered to diminish its global leadership role, and our self centered and unilateralist natures will assuredly make adjusting to more competitively attuned —less compliant—colleagues a challenging task.

Consider, for example, the new Pacific basin environment. For Asian colleagues, the value of post World War II American economic and security support has diminished. Indigenous manufacturing and trade networks have formed across the region, and the need for an American military presence to check Soviet Asian expansion is dead. With regionwide economic recovery and integration well underway and with disappearance of the revanchist Soviet threat, the Japanese electorate has ended the four decade long monopoly of the Liberal Democratic Party over domestic governance. The Cold War styled Yoshida doctrine died with that Party's 1993 electoral defeat, and an ideologically more left of center coalition government, one certainly less American deferential, gained governance authority. It is in the Japanese people's current interest to seek autonomous economic links with both the compatible markets of the Chinese Peoples' Republic and Russia. The bilateral exchange of Japanese high-end consumer manufactures and agriculture related technology for Chinese foodstuffs, primary resources and less sophisticated manufactures will be an assured early 21st century development. An exchange of ownership of the northern Kurile Islands—ceded from Russia to Japan—for application of Japanese technology in developing Asiatic Russia's economic potential might be a more alluring exchange for both states than would be any near term future Russian–American trans Pacific barter.

Also, consider the new trans Atlantic environment. Continental West Europeans are offering an enticing partnership to their East European neighbors. With a country to newly harmonize—east to west—, regional economic opportunities to seize and a lead role in the fifteen state European Union to fill, the Germans want to refocus their bilateral trans Atlantic relations. They need us less than they did when Kremlin policy controlled the East Germans and threatened their Western relatives. Most Germans are young enough to sense no personal obligations for the economic rehabilitation, physical security and absolution from wartime guilt which early Cold War America furnished. Germany's current condition makes sensible a rearrangement of trans Atlantic relations, and the late 1998 change in Federal governance indicates clearly the direction of that new relationship. The new Social Democratic - Green party coalition's focus is that of Germany the regional trend setter, not Germany the chief subordinate to one of two global bipolar power centers.

The Italian electorate has also selected new leadership from the ideological left center. The Olive Tree coalition, led by the successor to Italy's Communist party, governs largely because the Soviet threat is gone. Italians need no longer adhere to the right center coalitions compatible with American policy preferences and those of the Vatican. The new Italian agenda is economic enhancement, reduction of institutionalized domestic corruption and effective membership in the European Union. America has become less relevant—less vital—to the Italians' current needs.

The peoples and governments of Iberia, France, the Low Countries and Scandinavia were never obligated primarily to American policy preferences and priorities. While the larger states of Cold War Western Europe felt compelled to nurture strong assurances of American support, the smaller states—in tandem—"rode free." While remaining assured allies and partners, they could afford more overt exercise of their own interests. The sea change in temperament is in the peoples and regimes of Germany and Italy. They have eased off being America's "first string cheer leaders" and, in the post Cold War European climate, joined their "smaller" continental neighbors, leaving America to adjust to a diminished role regionally.

Only in our hemisphere are interstate relationships structurally unchanged. There are presently 23 million first generation Hispanic-Americans with somewhat permanent residence in the United States. As with all previous immigration waves, this one resides geographically clustered—providing assurance of a united voice. The exchange between their voice and that of mainstream America will heighten our attention within the hemisphere. Expanding market, banking and resource linkages will add to my country's interest in and dependance on its southern neighbors. Both through the North American Free Trade Agreement and the recent increase in bilateral public and private trade and financial agreements, the bonding is increasing. Additionally, concerns over illegal drug suppliers and users, over assumed inherent rights of humans living under repressive neighboring regimes and over the migration of economically destitute peoples northward across the Caribbean or Rio Grande will remain attention getting conditions. My country's news hungry media will keep those issues alive, feeding our hemispheric attention.

Yet, one hemisphere will not provide a sufficient playground for a people who believe they bear a right to the world, and many regional concerns truly have global seedbeds and consequences. We are responding equally to indigenous ethnic warfare in the former Yugoslavia and in Haiti. Our intelligence services track the flow of heroin not only across the Caribbean but also the Middle East. Heinous chemical weapons, in the hands of messianic groups, threaten all stable societies, and jobs and living standards in America depend on jobs and living standards not only across the hemisphere but throughout that global trade and financial network which we have nourished for half a century.

We Americans have always assumed a world ultimately shaped in our image. In the macro view, we believe that the best way of doing business, of relating in community and of building personal values is the American way. The rub comes when our success at peddling America's material benevolence takes hold, germinating or restoring not only the economies of client societies but also their original, temporarily dormant and not necessarily compatible cultural maps. This new relationship promises, in the early 21st century, to shock some smugly held American preferences and expectations. Perhaps, at this point, an advanced glimpse at the contemporary interaction between four American characteristics is helpful—a quick peek at how different the American value set or reference frame is from those of even our closest cultural neighbors.

Recall this: Doing competitive business—securing resources, manufacturing hard commodities, marketing and selling those products and financing the process—requires much innovation and pragmatic application. Because it has this "present centered" nature, doing business has always been an American strength. From agrarian to assembly line to high technology business, the American has competed successfully. Recall this: Successful business, as a primary social value, has fit the American demeanor because it is conducted ultimately for **personal**, comparative gain. Never have we Americans considered seriously any social structure or goal as superior in worth to **individual** enrichment. Recall this: Our "ecumenical" nature is as spontaneous as are our "self" and "present centered" natures. The objective is to make and sell better than others—not others of a given religious belief, ethnic background or other classification irrelevant to the marketplace as we view that "level playing field", but **all** others who can pay our price and thus contribute to our well being. We belong everywhere in this world.

Now, consider this: Until this 20th century's last decade, America had its way with the world. Throughout our first century, we chose to make external interests secondary to domestic ones. We were building enterprise at home. Throughout our second century, international conditions provided us first a recognized position among the most prosperous and influential states and then the position of undisputed leader. "Unilateralism" had to be embedded deeply in our cultural outlook. Yet, very recently, the ecumenical and unilateralist American experienced a changing international environment in which others are, for the first time, no longer submissive to our wishes. Others have become friendly colleagues who feel entitled to partnership. The internal logic of America's past way with the world—the four dimensional harmony between our self and present centerdness and our ecumenical and unilateralist natures—is collapsing as new interstate relations prove incompatible with those attributes collectively. Perhaps our self and present centered natures will provide some adaptability in the new climate, but global (ecumenical) involvement with an insistence on always having one's own way (unilateralism) will increasingly abrade interstate relationships in which no one partner can or is expected to dictate all terms of even his own condition.

A national character is not assured of harmony or cohesion between its traits. In all societies, today's harmonious characteristics become tomorrow's cultural contradictions. The next chapter will analyze the final dimension of the American global outlook. It is the one dimension which is not newly internally contradictory, but has provided a contradiction—frequently an abrasive—in our way with the world for two centuries. A **moral**, successful businessman may even be a contradiction in fact. Stay with me. The mosaic of America's character is incomplete without blemishes. The nature of one original contradiction is the substance of Chapter 6, and outcomes for the complete mosaic— America's upcoming fit globally—is the meat of my final chapter.

Chapter VI

The World's Moral Nanny

Birth of a Moralist

Revolutions, whether they throw off allegiance to a governing regime or fundamentally and rapidly change a nation's socio-economic climate, must be emotionally driven. The revolutionary community, both the leaders and the led, must feel the need for change from the heart as well as rationalize it from the head. It takes that dual commitment to risk and carry through on the destructive and reconstructive work which prerevolutionary incitement first told them was necessary. Additionally, the core dogmas which nurture revolution are not transient. They were disturbingly central to the revolutionists' thinking long before their call to action, and remained a central driving force in their lives long after stability was restored.

So it was with civil revolutions in 17th and 18th century Britain and France and in Wilhelmine Germany's and Meiji Japan's 19th century social reorderings for political and economic advancement. In like manner, a revolutionary fervor grew and then drove my people to challenge and then break from British rule. The kernel of that spirit also helped frame dominant post revolutionary outlooks in all five countries. It is by understanding the American revolutionary's spirit that you can understand and appreciate what that past code does for America's way with itself and the world today.

Perhaps the substantially moral nature of American revolutionary outlook can best be appreciated by asking four questions about its context vis-a-vis the revolutionary context once exhibited by the British, French,

Germans and Japanese. First, was the American revolutionary spirit—
and each of the others—simply a push for national economic or material
betterment? Second, how does my country's revolutionary fervor compare
as a means mainly to gain individual, as opposed to group—tribal,
community or national— betterment? Third, was the American
revolutionary way unique regarding the assumed universal applicability
of its moral credo? Fourth, revolutions can eminent from a belief that the
cause has a transcendent or spiritual validity—a moral justification from
God above humankind. To what extent was America's revolutionary
impetus, compared to the other national revolutions, of that nature? If
you appreciate the fit of the American 18th century spirit on those four
dimensions, you will understand the nature and importance of morality
in contemporary America's global style.

Admittedly, the wish to keep our earnings to ourselves, and to
compensate England as meagerly as possible for its support of our fledgling
growth, was a considerable factor in America's revolutionary fervor.
The belief that British rule stunted our affluence was widespread among
colonists. Mercantilism was the key to Britain's global grasp and
prosperity. Colonies, to include America, were to provide native raw
materials, those goods which were best produced in the colonies and an
exclusive market for the more refined British manufactures not absorbed
at home. Control over production and trade was the exclusive right of the
"mother country." British law restricted trans-Atlantic trade to British
vessels, required the export sale of American manufactures to Britain
alone and banned our manufacture of commodities which would compete
with those of England. Banking and currency control were exclusive
rights of the British government, and its Privy Council held an absolute
veto on any colonial legislative initiative. A debt ridden Virginia planter
whose cotton or tobacco crop faced continually declining prices, and
who was forced to buy British clothing and furniture by mortgaging his
future crops, did revolt substantially for economic reasons.

The 1763 Stamp Act—to beget tax revenue for the upkeep of 10,000
North America based British soldiers—precipitated colonial resistance.
The Act was repealed in 1766, but London's strained budget required
imposition of import duties on tea and other monopolistically controlled
items for colonial consumption, which led to smuggling and American
attacks on British shipping interests, which led to Britain's forced closure
of Boston port and other "Repressive" Acts, which led to war.

However, an economic causal train is hardly unique to the American bent for action. The 1860s-1870s German unification and Japanese modernization were mainly driven by economic concerns. By the 1860s, an entrepreneur spirit saturated the German business community. Alfred Krupp's iron works made Essen a company town, and the steel magnates of the Rhineland and Westphalia were in alliance with the Junker land barons of East Prussia to move the German confederation to the status of a great European power. The Zollverein, a tariff free union of the numerous principalities, provided the institutional framework. The will, diplomatic cunning and patriotic vision of Otto von Bismark gave the leadership. Over just seven years, the German confederation fought Denmark, then Austria, then France to forge economic ascendancy in central Europe. The revolution of "blood and iron" was a merger designed nearly totally to assure the German people of their share of the prosperity achievable in industrializing Europe.

As British enforcement of the Navigation, Townsend and Repressive Acts was America's economic goad to revolution, and bullying by neighboring French and Austrian regimes hastened the German confederation's merger for prosperity, so Commodore Perry's humiliating shelling of Edo harbor and the following introduction of American and British commercial interests into previously isolated Japan precipitated that nation's Meiji restoration. Perry's 1853 assault opened Japan to those exploitive trade relationships previously forced on the Indian subcontinent and China. The bombardment technique was repeated by the British in 1863 at Satsuma and on the forts of Choshu a year later. With the growth of western extraterritorial trade centers along its coast and imposition of tariff limits on Japanese exports, the Japanese leadership recognized their nation's need to rush into social and technical modernization. The alternative was economic and then political bondage. Pre Meiji Japan had been organized tightly around four classes; the ruler warriors at the top, followed by the peasants, the artisans and then the lowly merchants. Within three decades, the order was reversed. The Tokugawa shogunate and its Samurai warrior class were excised. The merchant houses of Mitsui, Mitsubishi, Sumitomo and Yasuda were set in control of a nationally networked banking, manufacturing, mining and transport structure. Perry's naval gunfire had precipitated a revolution in the Japanese outlook. An introverted and feudal society built on soldierly ethics was supplanted in three decades by the framework for a global economic powerhouse.

Possibly closest in motivational mix to the American revolution was the domestic upheaval which shattered the French monarchy just eight years after our Revolution's closing battle. The later German and Japanese gyrations were uprisings controlled by and retaining those states' senior pre revolutionary leaders, whereas—like the American experience—opposition to and destruction of the pre revolutionary seat of authority was a key factor in France. By the 1780s, fifty percent of the French state budget was absorbed by debt interest. A huge military expenditure and an extravagant lifestyle for the nobility and clergy were somewhat responsible for that outcome. Chronic war with England and the marginally productive use put to the 35% of land held by the nobility and clergy necessitated royal taxes and church tithes hoisted arbitrarily on the French "third estate"—peasants, artisans and those merchants who would or could not ally with France's ruling elite. A catastrophic grain harvest in 1788 starved the large farming community, and their consequent cutback in demand for manufactured goods impacted most small artisans and traders. Just prior to the march on the Bastille, one quarter of Paris's work force was unemployed.

Also, more like the American experience than those of the Germans and Japanese, hostility to economic conditions—although a necessary prod—was not sufficient cause to revolt. The late 18th century French and American revolutionary societies both believed deeply in the natural rights of man, and that those rights were being violated. In France, the National Assembly's 1789 declaration that "men are born and remain free and equal in rights . . ." with the inherent rights to "liberty, property, security and resistance to oppression" reflects an ethical focus conterminous with the prevalent American view. The Paris Parliament's nullification of Louis XVI's tax edict, on the eve of the march on Versailles, because of the citizens' "right to representation before taxation" again shows a parallel in trans-Atlantic attitudes—a mix of commercial and civil liberties bases for decisively changing things.[1] This second, non material, dimension to revolt will be reexamined as we uncover more unique aspects of the American moral temperament.

Unlike the other four uprisings, impetus for the British "Glorious Revolution" of 1688 was based only indirectly on commercial underpinnings. By the reigns of the last Stewarts—Charles and James II—the powerful British parliament represented England's commercial interests well, and achievement of prosperity and political influence had been open to Englishmen much more on the basis of talent and proven ability than was true across the traditionally feudal societies of continental Europe or Japan. Because there was no mercantilistic (colonizer to colony) or impervious feudal block to a gifted and energetic commoner's climb to wealth and domestic power, that issue was irrelevant in the British movement. The British revolution strove solely to retain at home Britain's control over its destiny. The church-state issue had been defined a century earlier, when Henry VIII severed the Roman Catholic church's direct influence from British governance. Yet, the Papacy and a faction within British nobility kept the issue alive. The last Stewart monarch was a devout Catholic. He attempted restoration of Papal control over what had become a very secular society, one which substantially favored governance through a representative parliament. James II stacked his Privy Council, the faculties of Oxford and Cambridge Universities and the Anglican (Church of England) leadership with loyal Roman Catholics. He imprisoned disloyal bishops in the Tower of London, and when his Italian Catholic wife delivered a male heir, Whigs, Tories, Anglicans, landed and merchant British elites united. The Glorious Revolution resulted in James's flight to Catholic France, the parliamentary determined establishment of Holland's William of Orange and his very Protestant wife Mary on the British throne and the firm establishment of a constitutionally circumscribed and Parliament controlled state monarchy. Unlike the American, French, German and Japanese revolutions, a recasting of the domestic economy was, at best, a tangential issue in England's most celebrated change.

In summary, we cannot conclude that a drive for material enhancement was unique to the American experience. Three of our four comparison societies also risked their lives and national futures for material gain.

Singularity of the American revolutionary spirit begins to appear as we explore the ultimate intended benefactor of our revolutionary experience. Unlike the British, French, Germans and Japanese—who erected new regimes to benefit entire communities within their societies, if not their entire nation collectively—the American challenge was and has remained essentially a revolution conducted for individual betterment. This ethical goal rested on religious and secular philosophies which sanctified the individual. Lutheran and Calvinist doctrine were deeply imbedded in colonial Puritanism: Luther with his emphasis on salvation available only through individual spiritual righteousness, and Calvin with his claim that self worth can be gauged by how productively prosperous a person is within the community. The Lockean model for just governance placed all **right** in the people—the national citizenry as a collective of **individuals**. Any institution erected to administer and hold authority over those people received its authority as a trustee only, and John Locke's perspective was the philosophic cornerstone of my country's regime formation. The beliefs of Charles-Louis de Secondat (Montesquieu) and Jean Jacques Rousseau influenced the American colonists greatly: Montesquieu who regarded logic and reason (individualistic attributes) as the only just bases for law or established social relations, and Rousseau who amplified Locke's reverence of the individual through use of a "social contract." There was no question as to the object being served by that contract when Rousseau defined good governance's only challenge to be "to find a form of association which will defend and protect with the whole common force the person and goods of each associate, and in which each, while uniting himself with all, may still obey himself alone, and remain as free as before."[2]

Clearly, Britain's Glorious Revolution was but one of a centuries long series of adjustments, by a majority ruling faction of that nation, to "fine tune" the apparatus of English governance, insuring material opportunity **for all citizens**. The traumatic French Revolution was a populist uprising of materially disadvantaged segments to expunge the authority and monopolized affluence of the established regime, and to redistribute that authority and wealth to the third estate **collectively**. The German confederation's unification trauma and Japan's Meiji Restoration were revolutions from above—by established elites who maintained their authority while remodeling their states' institutions **to benefit their entire national populations.** No one of the four European or Asian undertakings was designed to erect an authority structure which serviced the goal attainment of its entire membership **as individuals.**

We Americans were so protective of the individual citizen's autonomy that we fought our war for independence under a constitution which installed a committee as chief executive and prohibited central regulation of domestic commerce or taxing authority and averted a national judiciary—the Articles of Confederation. We testily submitted to a single executive authority only after revolutionary victory, only after serious post revolutionary uprisings in New Hampshire and Massachusetts made blatantly obvious the need for a strong central government, and after our wartime allies and creditors insisted that we "get organized" as a state. Even then the new supreme law clung to our love of the individual. More than creating a system of "shared powers," it established and insured one of "fractured powers"—a locomotive designed never to run away with its passengers. Federal authority was and is limited to prescribed activity, divided between three branches, set in an environment assuring interbranch competition and granting of law making and executing authority only to elected persons—public leaders whose job continuance is at the mercy of their electorates.

America's intended beneficiary was the citizen as an individual substantially because only the American, of the five societies, referenced a past free of a feudal order. The British pre revolutionary society, and more so those of France, Germany and Japan had long been organized by classes. Their revolutions were, by habit or tradition, one group against another—us against them. In contrast, the classless American colonists committed themselves to throwing off British governance only after positively answering the question "What's in it for **me**."

Again, on the third dimension revolutionary America forged a different outlook. We believed pervasively that we would uncover a code of community ethics bearing universal values, and erect a regime which— by example—would ennoble mankind. Our Declaration of Independence, the U.S. Constitution's justifying precursor, reflected blatantly that moral self assurance. "We hold these truths to be self evident, that *all Men* are created equal, that they are endowed by their creator with certain unalienable Rights, ...That to secure these Rights, *Governments are instituted among Men, deriving their just powers from the Consent of the Governed,*" etc. Few 19th century Germans or Japanese had a mindset to judge their aristocratic leaders—the German imperial family and Junker landowners or the Tokugawa and then Meiji Genro rulers of Japan. French commoners overthrew the Bourbon monarchy and France's Roman Catholic clerical leadership to end what seemed to be blatant inequities in lifestyle—not to introduce public management of government. After one short decade of social chaos, the French public eagerly subordinated themselves to a Corsican patriot—a dictator. Even the more independent minded English never intended to totally discharge their governing institutions. Of the five nationalities, they alone had repeatedly refashioned their regime to incorporate potential revolutionary elements.

The German unification and Meiji Restoration, the French Revolution and the Glorious Revolution in England were national endeavors. There was no intent to right wrongs against some universal truth, or to erect a regime model for global emulation. Only we Americans latched our revolutionary creation to such values. With strong moral self assurance and a sense of being exceptional, is it surprising that we are both ecumenical and unilateralist as well?

The source of our missionary bent is not hard to identify. Atypically, the secular and religious idols of America's founding spirit claimed to represent **universal** truths. Luther and Calvin championed the autonomous capability of **all** individuals, and Locke and Montesque espoused the natural law based fundamental rights and freedoms not of a class, nationality or religious synod, but of all people. Additionally, this universalist reference point was implanted in a community of "hyphenated"—multi ethnic—nationality. We were British or Scottish-American, French-American, Swiss and Dutch-American in the 1700s; Polish, Russian and Italian-Americans a century later and are Haitian, Mexican and Asian-American today. The three European and one Asian revolutions contained neither the universalist philosophical underpinnings to reference nor the multicultural populations to absorb such supranational principles with ease.

And, on the fourth dimension, we Americans do mix the secular and a more spiritual governance compass openly and often. We claim to separate religious orientations from our political arena, but find that separation doesn't happen. Although we are a denominational polyglot, each denomination's religious convictions are deeply held. The European settlement of America was as much driven by religious as by economic incentive. Anabaptists, Lutherans, Mennonites, Amish and splinter sects of Puritans each implanted its doctrine in pre and immediate post Revolutionary American lifestyles. The fifty five framers of our Declaration of Independence, representing a valid cut of 18th century American leadership, were schooled with deep religious conviction— John Adams from Puritan and Congregationalist Harvard and the Presbyterian Reverend John Witherspoon of New Jersey, who became President of Princeton. They were educated at Dartmouth (founded to train preachers for enlightenment of the Indian tribes), at Columbia (established to spread the Anglican faith), at Brown (which infused Baptist theology) and at Rutgers (a seat of the Dutch Reform faith). Our Declaration repeatedly referenced the backing of America's universalist God. "When . . . it becomes necessary for one People to dissolve the Political Bands which have connected them with another and to assume . . . the separate and equal Station to which the Laws of Nature and of *Nature's God* entitle them. . . . We hold these truths to be self-evident, that all Men are created equal, that they are endowed *by their Creator* with certain unalienable Rights. . . ." And in concluding our revolutionary justification, *"with a firm reliance on the Protection of Divine Providence*, we mutually pledge each other our lives, our Fortunes, and our *sacred* Honor. "

In contrast, the British Parliament sought little reliance on divine providence when it removed Catholic James and granted William of Orange the English throne. The Glorious Revolution contained little spiritual content, only a clear understanding by most Englishmen that self governance required excise of the Roman Catholic church's authority. The secular British monarch was to be undisputed head of a nationally autonomous Anglican ecclesiastical order. Over the decade between the storming of the Bastille and France's submission to Napoleon Bonaparte's dictatorship, leadership of the French Roman Catholic church—the dominant religion in that state—was vilified. In turn, the National Assembly, Robespierre's Committee of Public Safety and the Directory regarded the Church akin to the hated Monarchy. The French established their present day guarded outlook toward ecclesiastical authority during this transition period. Bismark's 1870s consolidation revolution bore almost no theocratic content. The German people had exited the Thirty Years War—in 1648—with a newfound revulsion toward the destructiveness of religious conflict. Over three short decades, one third of the German confederation's population had perished as Protestants fought Catholics for social dominance. After the signing of peace treaties at Muenster and Osnabrueck, the Evangelical Lutheran and Catholic clergy provided canalized instruction and support in societal civility—little more. Germany's 1870s unification was incited by economic factors and led by the German state's traditional and very secular elite class.

Only Japan's Meiji Restoration embodied a spiritual component comparable to the spiritual certitude which supported America's revolutionaries from Lexington to Yorktown. But, religion had a very different context and outcome in American and Japanese revolutionary undertakings.

True, the Shinto belief system provided the same propellant effect on Meiji Japanese society as the Puritan ethic had on American revolutionary firebrands. It gave an inner assurance of the rightness of their cause, and a roadmap for the revolutionary agenda. But, while Puritanism provided the early American a root belief in **his** capacity to change **his** environment through collective engagement, and a promise of **personal** material betterment if he won by the rules, Shinto beliefs focused Japanese **society**. Winston Davis identified four domestic communities which received this collective impetus. Shinto beliefs demanded of all commodity buyers and sellers credit worthiness, of entrepreneurs collectively the need for judicious risk taking, of investors a willingness to delay gratification and of industrial managers the right to have discipline in the shop.[3] Hence, both Puritanism and the Shinto outlook provided guidance on the revolutionary's justification and conduct, and both religious credos were enlivened by their role in the revolutionary movements. However, one credo identified the end beneficiary to be the national community, the other the individual.

Shuichi Kato, one of Japan's leading social critics, by defining clearly additional differences in the two peoples' moral outlooks, provides a contrasting structure to better understand morality's role in the American way. Under Shinto belief, God is heaven and earth. God is the mountains, sky and seas. Time is endless, seamless and repetitive in its processes. There is no universal set of principles for human interaction. Therefore, accommodation to group needs, unpatterned flexibility in ethical choices and adaptation to the condition's of one's environment are wise actions. Conversely, our Christian God **made** heaven and earth. God is transcendent of man , and made his son in man's likeness. The American God's universe has a linear and progressive agenda, a beginning (Genesis) and an ending (Revelations).[4] Therefore, the worthy Christian commits his individual energy to advancing personal and societal conditions according to one accredited guideline—his own perspective. The naturally assertive context of the American spiritual outlook goes far in explaining our self centered, ecumenical and unilateralist proclivities.

Puritanism, as a polestar for colonial activism, sanctified the individual—his natural rights and potential for governing his environment. It gave certitude that our morality represented universal right. Our morality's ennoblement of commercial endeavor provided the marrow for our founding Constitution. Then, an essentially uncontested and resource rich continental sized area sustained the environment necessary to reward assertiveness, reinforce our sense of being exceptional and validate our belief that the American way aligned with universal needs. Of the five nationalities, only the American has nurtured a moral justification for projecting his way on the world.

American Morality and the American Century

Luther's and Calvin's belief in the vitality and worth of the human sole was applied in individualistic early America. When, at Yorktown, we won our revolution, we instilled a constitutional order which fueled commercial development for the private gain of energetic citizens. The state-citizen relationships developed by Locke, Montesque and Rousseau were applied in late 18th and 19th century America. The vast and temperate southern half of the North American continent encouraged individual exploitive development largely without need to consider social accommodation, and geography and political relations between the major world powers benefitted our commercial and individualistic goals. Specifically, oceans to the east and west and comparatively weak neighbors to the north and south physically insulated America's autonomous growth. Europe's colonizing focus was on Africa, the Middle East and Latin America, and the interstate hostilities engendered by that race diverted the European colonizers from involvement in our nation's building agenda. In effect, for 100 years, no strong alternative challenged America's capitalistically focused and Puritan driven domestic growth. By the very late 1800s, we Americans had the resources to be a major power. We were also on the eve of circumstances which would grant our resource bank international leverage and were smugly confident that our comparative prosperity was both the result of our chosen growth agenda and deserved. Our way needed propagation.

Kato accurately identified the three circumstances which made the 20th century America's. First, the two global wars of the century's first half weakened the grasp and even the reach of all great colonizer societies except the American. At mid century, interstate friction shifted from mercantile (trade and manufacture) determinants to more ideological ones. We thus faced one competitor: the Soviet Union. The bipolar choice, for everyone else, was between market economic activity based on the rule of law and a centrally commanded economy based on rule by personality. The Soviet model became increasingly discredited, and, over the 20th century's latter half, America enjoyed an expanding world empire. Second, the growth of my country's imperial reach coincided with a geometric rate of growth in communication technology. The privately owned automobile, radio receiver, telephone, television and ham radio transmitter; then motion pictures, FAX, satellite relay and now the "information super highway" each has facilitated spread of the American culture across our empire. Third, the American culture is inherently multiethnic. It is, therefore, more proximate—more palatable—for adoption by other cultures than would be the mono cultures carried by the British, French or Japanese empire builders. The West and East European, the

African, the Latin American and Asian mass emigrations to America have resulted in most of the world having a cherished uncle in Chicago or San Francisco. Thus, the American way becomes more admissible.

In 1945, while defending U.S. ratification of the United Nations Charter, Senator W. R. Austin of Vermont stated," We recognize (in the Charter) that a breach of the peace anywhere on earth which threatens the security and peace of the earth is an attack upon us."[5] That statement mirrors the global commitment which Americans increasingly supported throughout the 20th century. We have carried our free market, national self determination and defense of individual rights mission into every continent, and have unilaterally backed the mission with military force. Until very recently, we applied our unique growth experience as proven remedy for foreign instabilities. From our Revolution through World War II, America overcame military challenges by postponing negotiation until recalcitrant opposition was subdued. Our Civil War was a fight to the finish, World War I ended with capitulation of the Triple Alliance, and the Second World War destroyed the Axis powers' social fabric. Undivided attention to the war fighting agenda and insistence on absolute victory on the battlefield are approaches consistent with a globally ecumenical, present centered people who prefer the unilateralist approach in executing their universal moral agenda.

The option of unilaterally postponing diplomacy until force crippled our adversary worked until the early 1950s, when it failed to deliver victory in Korea. Partial victory or strategic defeat then repeatedly beset America's use of force as a singular implement—in Vietnam, Lebanon, Somalia and now with questionable outcomes to our most recent Haitian and Balkan engagements. The proliferation and lethality of modern, conventional weapons arsenals and the existence of heinous weapons of mass destruction have curbed the policeman's latitude in wielding his billy club. A growing recognition that instability's causes are often not responsive to force based counters has frustrated the American penchant for absolute outcomes. Perhaps most disturbing to the American unilateralist is recognition that our treasured free market economic model often doesn't grow in different soil. Our devotion to a broad spectrum of natural rights for the individual is rejected by societies in which community needs are more pressing, and in which those rights are frequently inhibited by contrary cultural tenets. Additionally, our conviction that progress is linear, dependent mainly on the commitment of all individuals collectively and inevitable in the long term just isn't coming to fruition worldwide.

Our slippage in goal attainment is, for the first time, etching at the self assurance of this moral missionary society. In this book's final chapter, we will explore probable outcomes of this changing environment on America's way with the world.

Yet, American morality remains imbedded in all aspects of our approach to global relations. You should recognize that denominationally particular missionaries assertively contributed to our 19th century colonizing efforts throughout Asia and the Pacific basin. And today, America's sectarian missionaries are active throughout what were recently the agnostic or atheistic Soviet Republics and throughout Eastern Europe, some so noisy that their missions have been outlawed as destabilizing domestic factions. You should recognize that our Puritan belief that prosperity comes from individual commitment and assiduousness supports the correlate that those who are given an opportunity for personal improvement and fail to seize it deserve their poverty. And today, that reasoning justifies our parsimonious approach toward foreign aid to the least developed societies. The logic goes: "We've given before. They have used the gift badly or with apparent ill will toward us. They deserve their lot." America ranks among the least charitable states when foreign aid budgets are set against national GDP, and my Congress sets that policy because voting constituents actively condone—insist on—the position.

You should recognize that we Americans founded our nation as an experiment in better living for world emulation, and that, for nearly two hundred years, we sensed attainment of our values through adherence to that model. And today, one outcome of that rather smug approach has been the compartmentalizing or separation of foreign and domestic endeavors. We consider what is **inside** as perfectible and what is **outside** as needing very long term if not perpetual management. (The idea fits an ecumenical, unilateralist, doesn't it!) Because of our "us-them" reference point, we separate the institutions and processes for foreign and domestic policy making and execution. Our National Security Council is not staffed to include permanent expertise on the domestic conditions at play in supporting security policy. We erect a National Economic Council from expertise in the traditional domestic arena, but weak in permanent expertise on external conditions which impact constantly our domestic well being. We elect Presidents because they promise to shift the nation's policy focus **from** foreign **to** domestic agendas—implying that the coin's two sides are separable.

You should recognize that a moral mandate permeates the criteria which we use in judging our national leadership's performance. For example, we alone, of our comparison group's five nationalities, expect our President to both enshrine a personal life style which is morally exemplary and employ the cunning skills required to lead a global superpower successfully. The British demand the hardened values of a political leader from their Prime Minister, the nobility and humanity representing their nation's ethical values from their Monarch. In like manner, the German Chancellor manages state challenges and the President upholds the preferred national image, as do the Prime Minister and the Emperor for Japan. Even the French people offer their chief executive some latitude in juggling frequently incompatible roles by permitting their President to divest incongruous functions to a largely subordinate Premier. Only we Americans fuse the responsibilities and activities of Chief of Government and Chief of State—bad guy and good guy—into one elected office.

And today, our unwillingness or inability to acknowledge and alter the superhuman standard which the foregoing imposes on America's public leaders is in danger of eroding massively their job performance. With the deluge of new information sources available to most Americans and the recent introduction and public legitimation of "investigative reporting" as a media marketing tool, our insistence that all aspects of a senior official's personal moral background be disclosed is as much our interest as is our monitoring of his or her policy performance. Because the legitimacy of a senior civil servant to execute his or her job rests mainly on that person's image among constituents, the drum beat of both job and moral performance ratings becomes a killer. He or she leaves office early because some policy irrelevant personal indiscretion discloses the harassed official as less than saintly. Or the official acquires early a position neutral public stance on policy issues with a moral content. This erodes his or her dynamism to lead. Or the martyr attempts to set priorities on the performance under which he or she is being monitored—policy performance first and tangentially relevant moral deviations last. Yet, the moral dimension of the American character will not condone this last strategy, and the official's ability to be job effective is again reduced. The early termination of Henry Cisneros as Director of the Department of Housing and Urban Development exemplifies the first consequence. America lost a gifted and highly qualified administrator because of a non job related issue which may have besmirched his profile for no more wrong than an oversight. The 1999 media bombardment of Presidential candidate Bush on the issue of past (youthful) use of illegal drugs and of candidate John McCain concerning his position on the singular "Pro Choice–Pro Life" issue can only move both men toward habitual use of "safe" public statements—toward overcaution in performing the often controversial leadership duties of a President. Their experiences illustrate the second option available to a beset office seeker or holder. The lengthy investigative course applied to President Clinton's marital indiscretions and the heavy public reportage which accompanied those investigations illustrate the third option. Our elected Chief Executive's attention was nearly totally diverted, for more than a year in office, from a critical foreign and domestic policy agenda. The mystique necessary to nationally lead in the policy arena effectively was, in his case, savaged in the process of disclosing his personal, moral flaw.

The citizens of our four comparison nationalities most often overlook youthful or infrequent moral indiscretions in their leaders, if those indiscretions are job irrelevant. Those personal irregularities hold marginal public interest, and therefore make poor copy.

It is the American who is unable or unwilling to set job performance and private moral performance in priority because one's moral conformity is integral and equal in importance to job performance in American style leadership.

Back to the Old World Order

Until very recently, my patriotism was reinforced by having one believable external threat to my state. As a child, I had Adolf Hitler, Benito Mussolini and Hideki Tojo to fear. As a young student, Josif Stalin's regime was substituted. The Kremlin leader's threats against us and his policies of mishandling neighbors and America's friends were clear. His country was bigger that ours, and he was mean. As Nikita Khrushchev succeeded Stalin, then Leonide Brezhnev, Yuri Andropov, Konstantin Chernenko and Mikhail Gorbachev, each Soviet leader seemed a bit less threatening—more bumptious—than his predecessor. Gorbachev dismantled the East-West confrontation, and his more accommodating regime left me without a believable outside enemy. That has not been a totally secure atmosphere for me, or most Americans. Our polestar for calibrating America's moral purpose evaporated.

It was not difficult to lead a cohesive alliance when the Axis powers and then a globally active Soviet regime credibly threatened the political autonomy of many states and all democratic societies. There was much consonance between the dictatorial nature of those regimes, the paramount fears generated in America and most democratic nations and the style of American morality. Referencing those regimes, we could paint a believable picture of pure evil, generate a near sacred calling to repel the evil and assure ourselves that a single minded commitment to linear engagement was the sole route to victory—to absolute destruction of the malignancy.

We enjoyed abnormally bound allies. The validity, proximity and strength of the threat left physically smaller and weaker democracies dependent on America's enormous material capability in checking Axis and Soviet imperial designs. During the four decades long Soviet-American confrontation, some less developed nations would have preferred political neutrality. Yet, their need of domestic economic development required some external support. America was most able to supply that support, and made largess contingent on at least tacit support against Kremlin policy. For most of my lifetime, global political-security conditions have favored my people's cultural predisposition, that of an ecumenical, unilateralist with little attachment to our heredity—thus an ability to adapt strategic policy as changing security conditions dictated. Political-security conditions have favored my people's exercise of our moral perspective, enticing or coercing dependent allies to engage against **enemies** through military means and with total victory as the goal.

During most of my lifetime—from Franklin Roosevelt's Presidency midway through Lyndon Johnson's administration—the planning and management of America's way was direct, simple and appropriate for a people guided by a singular and self assured moral code. The President led the nation against our foreign enemies. Congress exercised proactive authority only in domestic issues, and we separated the foreign from domestic agendas absolutely. Nearly unquestioned Presidential leadership in foreign policy resulted from numerous circumstances. First, we sensed crisis, a genuine and imminent threat to our way of life, and America has consistently rallied behind its Chief Executive at those points in our history. Second, the belief was widespread that countering enemies led by dictatorial regimes required an equally rapid response authority. Within our Constitutional structure, only tacit subordination of legislative authority could provide that condition. Third, the Presidencies of the first half of the 20th century enjoyed the aura or mystique of being near prefect administrations led by highly energized, wise public servants. Change to the environment of "suspect leadership in a goldfish bowl" was discussed

previously. I only reiterate that our Vietnam conflict was the watershed
for change—for establishing an Executive-Legislative near gridlock and
such invasive public access to policy making details that policy movement
and continuity are greatly diminished today.

As America struggled to erect a viable native regime in South Vietnam,
failed and then experienced deep and widespread frustration in getting
out of the morass, the self debilitating perspective took seed among my
people: That the core cause of that war might not have been an attack by
evil North Vietnamese forces on those who we defended; and that our
approach toward overcoming the Hanoi regime's strategic goals—use of
technologically sophisticated and highly lethal conventional military
measures—might be ineffective at best, counterproductive to bolstering
the South Vietnamese cause at worst. It increasingly seemed that the two
Vietnamese sides did not hate each other as much as we were coming to
hate them both, and that the condition that caused their initial mutual
enmity—and our ultimate involvement—would not soon or easily be
responsive to American resources. Yet, we couldn't then comprehend
clearly what the war's cause was. We'd never before been in that
tractionless environment.

One short decade after our Vietnam withdrawal, the Soviet empire
began a rapid disintegration, and its atrophy ended the perception of
imminent threat both among our allies and among Americans. Our allies
needed us less. Consequently, they revised national priorities, returning
to those agendas—usually domestic or proximate—which concerned them
before the Soviet, and in some cases the 1940s Axis, threats. Many societies
readdressed religious or ethnic incompatibilities which had been suppressed
by two superpower overlords during the Cold War's bipolar faceoff.
They revisited chronic issues which had festered long before the American
century.

The fabric of global conditions now, for the first time in three quarters
of a century, mismatch expectations of the American moral outlook. We
now face vague dangers which slowly corrode our material values, not
evil enemies which are easily defined and defeated through direct attack
by force backed diplomacy or force itself. The just route to a conflict's
solution is no longer clear. Justice among ethnically or religiously warring
people is a relative, not an absolute condition, and the best short term
change that can be hoped for is a temporary stoppage of the overt slaughter,
with possible reconciliation through generational replacement. Even then,
routes to a cure are not linear. The warring communities have a multitude

of needs, and more than one avenue is open to an external enforcer and arbiter of peace in satisfying those needs and restoring civility in the region.

It isn't that we have abandoned attempts to have our morally particularistic way with the world. Although we have less self assurance than ever before, the particularistic messages of America's moral evangelists remain widely respected beacons available to our elected leaders. As noted previously, even candidates for national leadership must reflect service to those moral tenets to gain office. Is it surprising that this global hegemon is often regarded as the world's moral nanny?

Since our Vietnam experience ended, American frustration increased substantially because the moral components of our policies failed to take. In the early 1980s, we entered Lebanon to stabilize a community beset by factional warfare. We left in 1983, when 241 U.S. servicemen died in a bomb blast set off by one warring faction opposed to our intrusion. We entered Somalia a decade later, to grant civility to a society torn by feuding warlord bands. We left in October of the same year, after the ambush and killing of 18 American servicemen by one of the bands. Today, Lebanon remains a fracture zone, reacting to the kaleidoscopic shifts in Arab-Israeli relations, and the Somali population has no understanding of America's reason for entering their country with troops in 1993, much less our concept of a law governed society. The Castro and Kadafi regimes and Saddam Hussein's dictatorship still govern the Cuban, Libyan and Iraqi peoples, in the face of decades of American opposition to revanchist dictatorships.

My people are yet to accept fully the condition that American morality is not a universally accepted code—neither always applicable nor always wanted by alternative cultures. Henry Kissinger defines this short circuit in understanding as "the irrepressible American conviction that understanding between peoples is normal, that tension is an aberration, and that trust can be generated by the strenuous demonstration of good will."[6] We fail to understand fully that our singular success in building a stable and prosperous nation was as much the result of external circumstances which lasted a century and a half as it was the united effort of my people to do it. We fail to understand that smugly exporting our formula for success—in the context of a moral crusade—can be as intrusive on other cultures and their formative environments as is more physical invasiveness. And, our tendency to insist on the American way, applying economic and sometimes military sanctions in response to rejection of our missionary efforts, really profiles us as sanctimoniously domineering. Again, a Kissinger description of the America way: "That America defends principle, not interests, law, and not power, has been a nearly sacrosanct tenet of America's rationale in committing its military forces, from the time of the two world wars through the escalation of its involvement in Vietnam in 1965 and the Gulf War in 1991."[7]

America's attempts to bring peace and stability to Bosnia-Herzegovina illustrate vividly the forced fit between the American way and other societies' receptivity to our proffered support. In *To End a War*, Richard Holbrooke describes in detail how, over the 21 days of forging the Dayton peace accords, American principled goals clashed with the power interests of the warring parties inside and adjacent to the contested area. The mutually shared distrust and hatred between Croats, Bosnian Muslims, Bosnian Serbs and the Serbs of the eastern province have been centuries in the making—being founded on a litany of tragic personal losses, vendettas and counter vendettas. In shaping the agreement created at Wright Patterson airbase, American rationality for multiethnic peace constantly clashed with the overpowering felt need of three mutually hostile religious communities to each gain assurances of physical security and the lion's share of negotiated benefit. The American negotiators approached the process by refuting continued conflict as a sane option, by trying to germinate mutual respect and trust between the feuding parties and by expecting those parties to uphold the principle of "equity" as negotiated exchanges were discussed. Each of the antagonistic negotiating teams considered continued conflict a sounder alternative than abdication of any substantive terms. Relative prosperity and political stability at home and a position of global near hegemony granted the American team the latitude to negotiate on principle. We operate individually and collectively at A. H. Maslow's "esteem" and "self actualization" levels— on **principle**. Chronic and grinding poverty, neighborhoods and interpersonal relationships torn by ethnic bloodshed and genocide as a policy, and generations of frustration in the formation of a viable national identity forced on the Croats, the resident Muslims, the Bosnian Serbs and the Serbs of the eastern province the need to negotiate on **interests**. They—and most of this world's people—are suppressed to deal individually and collectively at Maslow's "physiological," "safety" and "belonging" levels.

The moral aspects of America's way with the world are seldom intended as self serving. They are the subconscious outcomes of the deeply moral context of our national founding, of our demonstrable success at creating an economically prosperous and politically stable society, of our belief that our national model is replicable beneficially worldwide and of our strong preference to spread the American way singlehandedly. However, when viewed from the perspective of a target of America's beneficence, the American way often becomes morally invasive of and insensitive to that recipient's own beliefs, proffered too frequently as a cloaked command rather than a suggestion without strings, and reflective of leadership that is a bit too smug (overbearing?) and naive concerning global conditions and capabilities. Obviously, being the world's moral nanny frequently does not enhance our image or policy effectiveness long term and worldwide. But then, our morality is one of five support timbers of our cultural framework. It is as immutable a shaper of our paradigm on this world as is American individualism and present centerdness, and our desire to impact the world and relate to it unilaterally. We are missionaries, and without our morality we have no mission. Without it, we are not Americans.

Suggested Readings

Davis, Winston, *Understanding Political Development*, 1987.

Kato, Shuichi, "Japan's Empty Core," in *At Century's End: Great Minds Reflect On Our Times*, Nathan Gardels (ed.), ALTI Publishing, La Jolla, 1995, pp. 198-213.

Holbrooke, Richard, *To End a War*, The Modern Library, N.Y., 1999.

Chapter VII

Stepping Through the Looking Glass

The Best of Times: The Worst of Times

Throughout the 1950s, 1960s and early 1970s most Americans assumed that victory over Soviet global influence would deliver America's military and economic preeminence worldwide. The assumption is understandable, first because the reward of undisputed global hegemony would justify the material sacrifices and energy expenditure of our early Cold War policies, and second because it seems reasonable to conclude that if there are two (superpowers), and one goes away, then there will be one. However, by the 1980s, that vision of global leadership was fading. The Kremlin's steady decline in external influence was not translating into a commensurate increase in Washington's influence. Then, with the collapse of the Soviet empire, America's economic and security related preeminence dissolved. My country's western hegemony had been depen-dent almost totally on the vibrancy of credible threat emanating from Moscow's imperial design.

Yet, America's transition to reduced global influence status will neither disappoint our citizens and leaders nor cause long-term reduction in America's desire to stay involved. By four years into the 21st century, we Americans will have accommodated to a role compatible with the small conflict ridden and economically interdependent world of 2004.

For the spring, 1994 issue of *The Oxford International Review*, I authored an article entitled "Security Challenges of a Lesser Hegemon."

In that article, I reminded readers that the American nation's commitment to Cold War polar leadership held no fantasized aim of cementing permanently our global domination. Temporary hegemony over the "anti Communist" coalition was regarded as a burdensome responsibility, unnaturally necessary to keep our level of personal well-being. Soviet imperialist policy was rated a paramount threat to that well-being. Upon overcoming the threat, if our wealth and its regeneration processes were in tact, a reduction in America's influence status for itself would be of little concern. I predicted, for the *Review's* readers, that the five traits analyzed throughout this book would both predetermine my country's post Cold War role and ease us into that role.

It is helpful, at this juncture, to review the change in international relations to which America must fit. Consider three distinctions, the Cold War environment to that of the very early 21st century. The three are not totally unique, one to the others, but there is sufficient difference between them that envisioning each relationship change singularly, then merging the three in your mind, will give a clear perception of how we attentive Americans view our imminent challenges. With that perspective, you will understand the basis for the policy agenda which I believe the American way is already fashioning in order to meet our fundamental goal—secure material affluence with individual liberty.

First, the global community is no longer compelled to at least superficially support the external policies of one of two regimes. During four decades of Cold War, Washington and Moscow did suppress effectively foreign and domestic intercultural hostilities of their client states. These hostilities were irrelevant or even destabilizing to advancement of the two polar powers' goals. For example, the Soviet Politburo conveyed that message, through Marshal Josep Tito, to the mutually antagonistic ethnic and religious factions of Yugoslavia. In like manner, Washington expected domestic harmony along its containment line—among the ethnic factions within Turkey, Iran, the Philippines and other multicultural allied states. Through substantial loss of sovereign autonomy by all but two states, bifurcated control maintained world order. Today, communities are resurrecting cultural identity preferences. International relationships have moved from a culturally unnatural binary structure to a spinning kaleidoscope more attune to ethnic and religious affinity. This change both rearranges the sources of interstate influence and disturbs global stability. With community based on cultural grouping, and with the cultural diversity present within and between states having dealings, friction and conflict on the intercultural fault lines is inevitable.

Now, with the Soviet empire changed to a region of mutually antagonistic ethnic factions—with the Kremlin's ability to extend influence and threat outward shattered—there is no need for America's past and culturally diverse clients to adhere to my regime's wishes. We cannot arrest reasserted religious and ethnic conflict until the warring factions mutually want us to. Somalia, Haiti and now the Balkan communities have demonstrated that loss in America's global grasp.

Second, the assets available to America, for influence enhancement abroad, are now either irrelevant to the wants of most foreign communities or available from alternative sources. Again, Maslow's needs hierarchy is useful in understanding the implications of present needs change. Throughout the Cold War period, both *physiological* needs and *safety* from Soviet control were our coalition partners' paramount interests. Food, shelter and health supplies continue as pressing needs in many of those nations, but the return of strong economies in Western Europe and Japan and the emergence of numerous somewhat stable other economies now provides many alternative sources for relief of the remaining destitute from physical want. Additionally, because economically destitute regimes can play one solicitous benefactor off against another, the givers have lost influence in enforcing conditions attached to their support. When America was the sole or predominant font of material support, we developed a model for the growth of healthy economies from weak ones, and we enjoyed a bilateral relationship which permitted us to press on our wards adherence to that model. We advocated early application of material support to creation and enlargement of diverse, indigenous private enterprises. The intent was to expand a middle class which was somewhat autonomous of traditional, usually authoritarian governance elites. The consequent enlargement of middle class tastes was to produce institutions erected to supply those tastes. Thus we sought erection of economically self sustaining and democratically inclined nations. In Southeast Asia and Latin America our recipe sometimes worked. Unfortunately, because the ruling regimes of today's ward states are able to shift or stack benefactors, each benefactor has little ability to enforce one model in use of its largess. Internationally aware Americans no longer envision development aid forcibly going toward development, but often as being siphoned off in greater magnitude to enrich the poor nations' pubic spokesmen—turned plutocrats. In Russia and contiguous states, this condition has served as a gushing umbilical to richly supply domestic organized crime, and has substantially sidetracked nationwide economic recovery. It is a very possible and worrisome outcome for China and many fledgling nations in south Asia as they more independently order their national environments.

Belonging, a higher order of need, now substitutes for the Cold War era *safety* need felt keenly by most of our former colleagues. With the Soviet menace dissolved, people most want to be with "their own kind," and those clusterings generate strong ethnic and religious consciousness, then heightened awareness of invented or real inequities in land or resource distribution—one ethnic group to an interacting one. The fissures between Mindanao's Islamic community and the rest of the Philippine nation, between the Catholic community of East Timor and the remainder of Indonesia, between Pakistan and India, Tibet and China and the Balkan polyglot of cultures each generates salient global stability problems, largely because the lower order safety need of the bipolar arrangement is no more. And, Americans relate poorly to today's ethnic or religious cravings and goals. Our western cultural composition and attendant prescription for attaining material affluence are outside their referenced agendas—often blunderingly intrusive preachings when we intervene.

Third, the interstate clustering pattern has not only shifted from a bipolar to a multipolar arrangement and from one based on the dictates of physiological and safety needs to physiological and belonging needs, but a base pattern in which regional grouping of type nations is appearing. America's economy, ecumenical nature and commitment to ceding our moral code compel us to favor and champion a globally inclusive interchange between states: a free-market manufacturing, trade and finance structure free of regional barriers. Yet, Samuel Huntington's global mosaic of abrasively competitive multi state cultures, described in his national best selling book *The Clash of Civilizations and the Remaking of World Order*, seems to be congealing.

In Huntington's projection, four dynamic "civilizations" are rapidly emerging. The "West," predominantly Atlantic community of central and western European states and North America, most frequently acknowledges United States leadership. The "Orthodox civilization," led by Russia, is a block of contiguous nations of eastern Europe and extreme western Asia. The "Sinic civilization" of eastern Asia is increasingly responsive to Beijing's wishes, whereas the fourth dynamic civilization—"Islam"—differs from the other three in having not yet accepted one state regime as leader. Islam's unique lack of geographic cohesion adds to its aggressive nature. Other distinct civilizations—Latin American, Sub Saharan African, Japanese, etc.—are increasingly playing supportive roles to one or a combination of the four, mainly because of the expansionist nature of the dynamic four's cultures and the vastness of their physical assets.[1]

Huntington envisions considerable early 21st century friction and hostility within both Sinic-Western and Islamic-Western relations—the former substantially because of China's increasingly global reach, and the latter because of a multitude of demographic and economic problems.[2] I do not believe that the West, most notably the United States, will project durable or deep hostility toward China. There will be misunderstandings and name calling at the official, diplomatic level, and China's continuing increase as a manufacturing and trade competitor will generate vaguely targeted hostility among America's industrial wage earners. However, no living American generation has regarded the Chinese society as a sworn enemy of our well-being. Until post Mao regimes began China's methodical but energetic assent to a world economic power, Americans largely considered the mainland Chinese society a sometimes ally or, at worst, an ideologically misguided upstart. During the Cold War's height, with widespread pubic support, my government established a rapprochement with Communist China—a counter to Soviet Asian influence. Chinese military assertiveness, over the past half century, has been regarded as solely regional—seeking objectives of territorial adjustment along its Soviet border, over Kashmere and Tibet, and with India, Vietnam and Taiwan. Additionally, two communities with very strong influence over American public and elite attitudes toward China will keep my people's view of the Chinese society and regime essentially positive, our Western allies who do not hold the economic based anxiety prevalent in America and the massive populations of overseas Chinese whose emotional attachments to their cultural homeland remains strong. Within the larger community of states, Chinese policy generally is regarded as responsible and, beyond East and South Asia, comparatively benign.

I am not predicting pervasively amiable official relations between the United States and China over the next decade. China's assured rise as a leading economic influence globally will stir a pique across affected American sectors. Its economic maturation also makes plausible an increase in China's military power projection. National prosperity translates to increasing international contacts—with both negative and positive consequences—and more resources for a military buildup if considered appropriate. However, past performance hints at very controlled power projection targeted solely along China's borders, and a global expansionist agenda considerably less unilaterally assertive than were those of Britain, France, the United States, Germany and Japan when they experienced a domestic industrial revolution.

The combined impact of four conditions forces me to predict America's near term future relationship with the Islamic "civilization" to be our most unstable, most hostile one. First, the rate of population growth among Islamic communities is invariably higher than that of Judeo-Christian, Orthodox or Sinic populations. The economic, political and social disruptions inevitable in this increasing ethno-religious imbalance will insure continuing upheaval in the former Yugoslavia, Russia, the Philippines and numerous other bicultural and multicutural states and regions. The upheavals will cause American official and public involvement. Second, similar to the recent past relationship between the core Capitalist and Communist ideologies, Christian and Islamic beliefs are too mutually contentious to be other than troubled. We both believe in our own, transcendent God, believe our theology to be the preferable global way, are zealous in spreading our way, and we hold incompatible teleological goals. Third, inflamed divisions within the Islamic civilization will spur their hostility toward all non Muslim societies. Unlike the Western, Orthodox or Sinic civilizations, there is no single leading Islamic state or nation which the others have agreed to follow ideologically. Secular, moderate and religiously zealous regimes will each ply its unique foreign and domestic policy agenda to both maintain domestic stability and gain influence ascendancy within the civilization. This competition has to keep the global pot stirred up, with my country fulfilling the dual and oft incompatible roles of jaded "honest broker" and status quo defender. Fourth, no major civilization has been more colonized than were the tribes professing present day Islam. That recent past condition provides an easily combustible basis for triggering inter civilization hostility. Furthermore, within the Islamic world, American recent past foreign policy is regarded as having been equally imperialistic to those of the traditional European colonizers, and America today is repeatedly branded the sole remaining global neocolonialist—the foreign force using indirect economic levers of influence in the absence of more direct colonial rule.

From the American perspective on this turn of the century world, Robert Art's label of the global environment seems justified. Substantially, we Americans are in the "crazies" era. We acknowledge increasingly the need to adjust to an influence alignment in which we have recently diminished global leverage, but in which we need those others as much as we did during our Cold War "heydays" of influence. Relationships which are responsive, reliable and rewarding to us are necessary in delivering our one core value—widespread material well-being in a personally lightly encumbered, stable and secure national setting.

Impact of the Traits

The five anchoring traits of America's way with the world, and their supporting institutions, have mutated little in response to our changing environment. Each is necessary in anchoring our unique national character and identity and in keeping us materially advantaged and secure. Consequently, they will again shape our responses to upcoming change in international relations. How will the five interact in this new world relationship? What American policy patterns can be expected? Will the outcomes benefit or degrade American prosperity, individual liberty and security? What impact will our style have on other societies?

The American's **present centered** nature can only advantage my peoples' pursuit of continued material well being. The world community is assured of interstate power shifts as old ethnicities and particularistic religions reemerge as community organizing polestars, as economic activity merges in a supra state context and as we all accommodate to a geometric increase in technology's influence on life. Those societies least wed to tradition, habit and custom for their own sake are best postured to mutate beneficially. Friends and enemies alike have characterized our values as shallow, transitory, Philistine, utilitarian. Comparatively, the American's present centered nature projects all of those qualities, and therefore aids us in discarding past opinions and attendant agendas to better protect our one immutable set of values.

The focus of America's attentive public and public leadership is now on domestic concerns. It will remain largely domestic for some time, and akin to our 1920s and early 1930s focus, the basis for introspection will in no way signal isolationist sentiments. It will again reflect clear and widespread recognition that we can best use available assets at home. In the 1920s, that domestic engagement was to capitalize our public into an emerging industrial and financial network. Today, the reengagement is to refit our workforce from smokestack or assembly line to technology based pursuits and to regenerate resources which have been drained by half a century of global commitment. However, unlike our 1920s outlook, Americans now more appreciate the interconnected nature of domestic and foreign interests and policies. As we retool at home, the alignment of external conditions to benefit the domestic retooling will be a conscious endeavor.

One could sense the swing toward domestic concerns when a war hero President lost his bid for a second term because his leadership image was too devoid of expertise and activity at home. George Bush the senior ambassador, Central Intelligence Agency Director and brilliant military commander-in-chief was too "type cast" for our public's sudden shift in interest to the home front. One can also sense the swing as America identifies new "public heros." During the Reagan administration, the foreign policy wishes of State Secretary Schultz and Defense Secretary Weinberger dominated our media messages. Now, following a four year transition administration, the micro managers of our domestic economic and legal environments—Alan Greenspan and Janet Reno—more command the attention of America's electronic and print media. One can sense the groundswell of public demand for change in the impatience reflected by our electorate over the pace of policy change. When it wants policy change, the voting American public does not know specifically what it wants, but it does know and indicate to elected leadership that it does not like what it has. It sets the pace for such change by threatening the stability of institutions which grant elected leaders long incumbency. Our two party electoral structure is such an institution, and the frequency of challenge to that structure is growing. A third party challenge every dozen years is unusual, and it indicates clearly my peoples' commitment to having change.

The increasing strength of that third party threat indicates as clearly our growing impatience with the pace of change. George Wallace's 1970s challenge had too regional a loyalty base to provide other than a goad. John Anderson's 1980s challenge was national in recruitment, but "light weight" in image. Ross Perot's Reform party now includes the leadership of Pat Buchanan and Donald Trump, two personalities with higher national images than those of the previous system challengers. The Reform party has developed as comprehensive an issue based platform as those of the Republicans and Democrats. A third party will not become my country's early 21st century source of elected leadership, but the growing influence of a third alternative projects clearly the willingness of American society to threaten any process—the two party institution in this case—if it hesitates in delivering their sought after product—in this case, leadership which delivers major domestic policy change.

Over the 21st century's first decade, significant change will be made in the costs and coverage programs for public health care delivery, in the content of America's public K-12 educational curricular and in modes of passenger and goods transportation within the contiguous 48 states. The three activities are widely acknowledged to need repair, and—in their very late 20th century condition—to be detriments to America's well being. Abandoning a past pattern, my country will not implement a post Cold War reduction in its worldwide military commitment or an appreciable decline in our Defense department's share of the annual budget. The standing force structure of all four services will be restyled, from large units designed for effectiveness in traditional conflict environments, toward smaller units which can autonomously be effective in low intensity conflict. New weapons systems will incorporate ease of transportability, stateside materiel concentration will supplant dependence on foreign positioning and quick air and sea lift capability will be substantially enlarged. In summary, our present centered nature will drive us to create and implement an agenda designed to reenergize America's global influence grasp from a revitalized domestic base.

Although it will abrade relationships, we Americans will continue to act **unilaterally**. Our determination to preserve domestic material well being in a world of scarcity, our belief in the "rightness" of our purpose and our possession of the assets necessary to sometimes compel others will assure that solo posture. Our economic policy reflects that approach— the Helms-Burton law's counter to other states' trade with Cuba and our statutory treatment of bilateral trade relations with both Japan and China being examples. Our near solitary refusal to ratify the 1998 land mine treaty or the 1999 nuclear non proliferation treaty evidence America's covetousness of autonomy in security matters. The level of our commitment to international organizations will be directly proportionate to our perceived influence over them—the United Nations, the International Monetary Fund and World Bank, the World Trade Organization and operating alliances. We somewhat expect those organizations to approach global economic and security problems largely in tandem with America's somewhat changeable approach.

This egocentric stance will generate international misunderstanding and interstate irritations. Relations between Americans and others will hinge largely on how well those others understand the American character and motivations—ultimately, how much affinity and cultural commonality we share. Consequently, early 21st century relations between Americans and the Europeans and English speaking nations outside Europe will continue essentially harmonious. We will work out our comparatively small differences equitably. We will develop and keep essentially compatible relations with the Orthodox nations of southeastern Europe, the former Soviet Union and Catholic Latin America. China's political development and global economic emergence will cause binational frictions, mainly as we interact over south and east Asian interests. However, those sustained tensions will not precipitate conflict for reasons cited previously. Again, America's most troubling relationship will be with the Islamic community. The prior cited causes of friction will be mutually manageable between us and moderate Islamic regimes, prone to ignition of low intensity conflict in our relations with insecure regimes plying particularistic religious missions.

Yet, out unilateralist predisposition will be somewhat restrained by three considerations. First, we American's acknowledge interstate economic interdependence to be a key source of our physical well being. Second, we acknowledge the diminishing utility of America's use or threat to use force. We acknowledge the lack of responsiveness of big problems to that remedy, and the dangers inherent in armed conflict fought with today's weapons inventories. Third, we have become essentially the defender of the international status-quo, and prefer the stability accorded by some compromise to the unknown consequences of always pursuing unfettered self interest worldwide.

Aspects of the way in which Serb occupied Kosovo was returned to an essentially Muslim population provide a preview of America's future peacemaking style. Anxiety over the potential for regional spread of the war between Orthodox Serbs and Islamic Kosovans, a felt need to demonstrate—to such moderate Islamic populations as the Turks and Egyptians—the "honest broker" intent in our peacemaking activity, and a moral compunction to stop genocide in the heart of the Balkans each contributed to our leading a multinational effort which forced the withdrawal of occupying Serb forces and encouraged return of displaced Kosovans to their homes. Although America's action ran contrary to the tendency of nations to target support by cultural affinity, America's commitment to right a claimed wrong had limits. Our protracted method of forcing a Serb withdrawal provided them time—before their withdrawal—for retribution on the Kosovan population who had not fled, and we gave little rehabilitation support once the displaced Kosovans returned to their homes. The lack of American resolve to administer justice for all warring factions was again demonstrated when we demurred in checking returning Kosovans from indiscriminate retaliation against those few Serbs who did not flee—Serbs who had been non aggressive neighbors throughout the period of hostility and were as entitled to remain in Kosovo as were the returning Muslims. Yes, we Americans will continue to choose our options largely alone. First, we always have done so. Second, we are big enough to resent external constraint. Third, being unilateralist and satisfying the core goal of domestic well-being have previously been a compatible approach and objective.

Manifestly, my peoples' **ecumenical** worldview has fueled American involvement globally. American industry's early 20th century creation of a global market overtly placed us everywhere. The 1944 Bretton Woods agreement, making America the center of the non Communist world's trade and its banker, codified our entanglement. America's creation and then modification of the multinational corporate structure into an institution governed most frequently through multinational boards of directors sealed our interdependence.

However, one must not link America's ease with worldwide involvement with preference for a multicultural society domestically. Professing the right to influence foreign societies does not necessarily legitimate cultural diversity at home. The two were not paired conditions in the home societies of Roman, Iberian, Dutch, French or British imperial states, and they are not with us Americans today. In fact, our increasing commitment to repair domestic institutions in order to restore national vitality for global application will incline us to favor the ethic of domestic cultural homogeneity. Simply put, American "correctness" will increasingly resemble the core founding code of our economic development period: the Puritan ethic. The "work ethic" will be heralded, "entitlement" discredited. Public welfare programs in "affirmative action"—programs which introduced school bussing and the hiring and acceptance of ethnic minorities by favorable quota—will end. The increasingly exclusionary content of American immigration law, the sharp decline in national legislation designed to improve the lot of disadvantaged resident groups, California's negation of ethnic minority entitlement benefits and the persistent campaign to charter English as our nation's only official language are indicators of American society's movement toward cultural homogeneity. Perhaps with some irony, the American's deep seated appetite to be everywhere and influence all cultures is a major source of our need for harmony at home—clear, self identification. Awareness of and immersion in the world's cultural diversity fuels our push for domestic cultural uniformity.

Because a collective **self interest** is the core motive and organizing principle of America's energy, all early 21st century policy will be framed to honor that egocentric focus. Policy changes in public health care delivery, public education's content and the efficiency of transportation networks will be made because the perceived misfocus or dated nature of our present programs is considered a direct drain on our ability to compete internationally for national—translated "my"—well being. Within the next decade, we will substantially modify America's electoral campaign funding processes because of growing public rejection of a process which is widely regarded as filtering exposure and open discussion of public issues considered personally important—a block to satisfaction of self interest. Possibly a rewrite of the 1974 Presidential Election Campaign Fund Act and its amendments to include members of Congress, to cap the escalating cost of seeking elected national office and to preclude extreme differences in resources available to candidates.

Although the foregoing agenda for policy change is domestic in content, one should remember that it will be intended as a means of rejuvenating our reach and grasp worldwide—as rejuvenating of the tools which we believe essential to delivery of *my* material well being. Additionally, pluralistic routes to retooling do not translate to our automatic defense of democracy in foreign environments. America's Cold War era allies were chosen because they were anti Communist regimes, not because they were democratic ones. Our current close associates remain such because their economies and ours link beneficially, not because their regimes are public participant ones. We will enter the 21st century the strongest state proponent of a global free-market economy. We need an essentially open, global trading system to sustain prosperity across our continental sized nation. We will encourage growth—within the national economies of trading partners—of private enterprise. Privatized national economies most align with the globalized fiscal, manufacturing and trade networks favored by America's business leadership. Their regimes' level of domestic pluralism is of secondary concern to Americans.

At first glance, our penchant to preach America's **moral code** as a universal imperative while blatantly favoring—in policy—interacting regimes on the sole basis of their economic utility to us might seem a deceitful demeanor. Yet, advocating the supremacy of the individual, the rule of law, opportunity equality and the representative form of government which serves those principles will remain an American script. Nor will we reduce the missionary zeal we display in propagating this paradigm because global espousal of American morality provides the cognitive justification of our own societal ordering—the advertised defense of our quest for *personal*, material advantage encased in a secure home environment.

In proselytizing our moral code, we seldom consider its disruptive impact on the delicately balanced institutional networks of other societies or its challenge to contrary moral codes erected to serve different cultures. We encourage its adoption by others not only to legitimate our domestic social order, but also because all people prefer others to become like them—the better to understand them—the better to reason with and influence them. Thus, attempts to create convert societies are partly America's conscious intent to increase our global grasp and partly the subconscious self-defense of an outlook which was centuries in the making. America is the capstone inheritor of Western civilization's organizing principles—to include the legitimation of imperial influence. Today, the defense of national interests is regarded as the highest legal right, and America's vital interests are demonstrably global. Yes, my German father-in-law spoke sincerely and reflected a prevailing view among people socialized outside the United States when he remarked, "It isn't your hypocrisy which we Germans find most frustrating. It's that you Americans believe the hypocrisy."

Predictably, the moral accompaniment to America's foreign relations will be received most positively—with considerable understanding and agreement and some amusement—by Europeans and the English speaking peoples apart from Europe, less by the nationals of Orthodox Eastern Europe, often begrudgingly by East and South Asia's "Sinic civilization," and often with open or barely masked hostility by the diaspora of "Islamic civilizations." Islamic codes and American moralism will offer abrasively competitive rationales for organizing global assets and reinforcing the influence grasp of their respective practicing communities.

Back to the Future

America's preeminent global grasp will not be eternal, but over the 21st century's first decade it will prevail. We Americans now recognize the symbiotic relationship between our nation's global involvement and our level of material affluence and personal security at home. The joint influence of the five deeply imbedded national characteristics will commit us to an internationalist posture with enthusiasm. The focus of new policy will be domestic principally because we believe our domestic environment to be most in need of repair.

The informed populations of this world will largely regard the American as the best of a poor choice of available hegemonic influences. That world will consider America's way with them as being self serving—as doing what is best for America in a material and utilitarian context. Their reasons for cautiously maintaining positive linkages with America will rest on the condition that their national or regional need for stability and prosperity parallels America's global need for the same environment. Thus, the dual functions of *defender of the status quo* and *jaded honest broker of last resort* will support our preeminent influence for a decade.

As my country pursues its interests, the one trait on which we will reluctantly most accommodate is our unilateralist preference. Clearly, with the economic fusion of today's great state economies, the lethality of pervasively available weapons inventories and the nature of tribal or community instabilities, no one state can hope to dictate international policy from a hegemonic position. Our present-centered nature will, on a case-by-case basis, incline us to share leadership or undertake secondary roles within a multinational team effort when the perceived consequences of such a role do not appear injurious to America's basic national interests. Probably to the long term detriment of our preeminence in exercising global influence, the particularistic and missionary natures of the American moral outlook will force us increasingly to favor like cultural nationalities in our foreign exchanges. Probably with damage to long term world stability and economic development, deep American cultural preferences will keep Samuel Huntington's warning of a global condition of *the West against the rest* a real and present danger.

Yet, we Americans will remain what we always were: A present and self centered people who prefer unilateral approaches to the multitude of challenges to which our ecumenical outlook commits us. In addressing those challenges, we will continue referencing a deeply held set of moral codes which are culturally particularistic—arguably the apogee of the Judeo-Christian code funnelled into a Puritan ethical charter. For the next decade, that character frame will be America's way with the world. It cannot change appreciably, for if it did, we would no longer be Americans.

Endnotes

Preface

1. Kissinger, Henry, *Diplomacy*, Simon & Schuster, c. 94, p. 803.

Chapter 1

1. Shatrov, Mikhail (playwrite), as cited in David Remick's *Lenin's Tomb: The Last Days of the Soviet Empire*, Vintage Books, c. 94, p. 71.
2. Kissinger, Henry, *Diplomacy*, pp. 701-702.
3. Almond Gabriel & G. Bingham Powell, Jr., *Comparative Politics Today: A World View*, 6th ed., Harper Collins, c. 96, p. 36.

Chapter 2

1. Tocqueville, Alexis de, in Thomas Dye & Harmon Zeigler's *The Irony of Democracy: An Uncommon Introduction to American Politics*, 8th ed., Brooks/Cole, c. 90, p. 339.
2. Dalton, Russell in Almond & Powell's *Comparative Politics Today*, p. 276.
3. Dye, Thomas & Harmon Zeigler, *The Irony of Democracy*, pp. 227-230.
4. Manley, Michael, in Nathan Gardels' (ed.) *At Century's End: Great Minds Reflect on Our Times*, ALTI Publishing, c. 95, p. 265.
5. Kennedy, Paul, *Preparing for the Twenty First Century*, Random House, c. 93, pp. 290-349.
6. Huntington, Samuel P., *The Clash of Civilizations and the Remaking of World Order*, Simon & Schuster, c. 96, pp. 32-33, 183-206, 245, 301-312.

Chapter 3

1. Tocqueville, in Arthur M. Schlesinger, Jr.'s *The Disuniting of America: Reflections on a Multicultural Society*, W.W.Norton, c. 92, p. 25.
2. Davis, Ann, in Ramsay Cook's *Canada, Quebec and the Uses of Nationalism*, 2d ed, McClelland & Stewart, Inc., c. 95, p. 202.
3. Cook, Ramsay, *Canada, Quebec and the Uses of Nationalism*, p. 198.
4. Bailey, Thomas A., *The American Pageant: A History of the Republic*, 3d. ed. D.C.Heath & Co., c. 66, pp. 788-790.
5. Arbatov, Georgi in Charles Kegley & Eugene Wittkopf's *World Politics: Trend and Transformation*, 6th ed. St. Martin's Press, c. 97, p. 90.

Chapter 4

1. Lowenthal, Abraham, in Robert J. Art & Seyon Brown's *U.S.Foreign Policy: The Search for a New Role*, Macmillen Publishing Co., c. 93, p. 359.
2. Mastanduno, Michael, in Art & Brown's *U.S.Foreign Policy*, p. 136.

Chapter 6

1. McKay, John P., in Bennett D. Hill & John Buckler's *A History of Western Society*, Vol. II, 3d ed., Houghton Mifflin Co., c. 87, p. 680.
2. Rousseau, Jean Jacques, excerpts from "The Social Contract", in William Ebenstein's (ed.) *Great Political Thinkers: Plato to the Present*, 4th ed., Holt, Rinehart & Winston, Inc., c. 69, p. 454.
3. Davis, Winston, "Religion and Development: Weber and East Asia Experience," in Myron Weiner & Samuel Huntington's (eds.) *Understanding Political Development*, Little, Brown & Co., c. 87, pp. 221-279.
4. Kato, Shuichi, in Nathan Gardels' *At Century's End*, pp. 204-205.
5. Scigliano, Robert, in David A. Deese's (ed.) *The New Politics of American Foreign Policy*, St. Martin's Press, c. 94, pp. 161-162.
6. Kissinger, Henry, *Diplomacy*, p. 770.
7. *Ibid.*, p. 477.

Chapter 7

1. Huntington, *The Clash of Civilizations*, pp. 238-245, 272-291.
2. *Ibid.*, pp. 103-121, 209-245.

Glossary of Terms

ALIENATION: An attitude of mental or emotional non support. A person can be as passively *alienated* as to deny that interacting people or conditions are relevant to their lives or of interest to them or so actively *alienated* that they fight for destruction of the *alienating* source.

ASCRIPTIVE (versus ACHIEVEMENT BASED) LEADERSHIP: Two quite different approaches in leadership selection. *Ascriptive* style leaders are selected on the basis of one or a few traditional, usually positional, criteria—in theocratic regimes, the senior cleric of a state's dominant religion, and in many secular societies, the eldest male heir to a deceased or incapacitated monarch. Regimes managed by *achievement* based leaders select those leaders through processes determined to best identify and test needed leadership assets. The assets sought vary over time as the state's perceived needs change.

AUTARCHY: A condition of community self sufficiency—not being dependent for its well-being on reciprocal relations with other communities. The term usually references a state's economic or physical (security) independence. Actual achievement of a condition of *autarchy* would enhance a state's ability to either leverage other states or isolate itself from its surrounding environment.

AUTHORITARIAN (versus PLURALIST) REGIME COMPOSITION: *Authoritarian* regimes determine leadership from within a small, elite segment of the governed population. Policy is then developed and implemented by that elite, without meaningful mass public influence. Within *pluralist* regime structures, multiple and competing institutions with "grass roots" public legitimacy both determine public leadership and generally frame the policy agenda to be executed by that leadership.

COGNITIVE DISSONANCE: Societies remain stable largely because their citizens interact using established behavior patterns. Reward and punishment, occupational success and failure, respect and disrespect, these results are consequences of adhering to or deviating from the expected behavior norms. However, when basic social values change or new ones are forced on a society, new norms of interaction are required. Expectation or predictability in interaction is lost—becomes discordant. The battle for supremacy between old and new values—and the consequent loss of predictability in interaction—produce societal discord or *cognitive dissonance*.

ECUMENICAL: An attitude of assumed right to enter or intrude into the working of all societies, worldwide. The attitude (as used in this book) does not incorporate either an acceptance or a closed view toward other cultures, only the right and need to intermingle one's own cultural approaches with all others.

HEGEMONY: Domination of one state's economic and/or physical power by another—by the *hegemonic* state.

NATION (versus STATE): Any community having a sense of mutual kinship or affective linkage constitutes a *nation*. Shared language, religion, secular customs each contributes toward this affective, cohesive climate. The legal and institutional structures with authority over a citizenry and within a designated territory constitute a *state*. Under international law, the state is the ultimate sovereign within its territory.

"OSTPOLITIK": Initiated by the German Federal Republic's Willy Brandt government, in the early 1970s, *"Eastern Politics"* assembled and executed a foreign policy agenda seeking trade and social liberalization between the Federal Republic and all states of the Warsaw Treaty Pact. To varying degrees, the agenda was adopted by all West European and North American governments, and is widely considered to be one major cause in the Cold War's peaceful reconciliation.

PARLIAMENTARY (versus PRESIDENTIAL) REGIME STRUCTURE: Both structures imply pluralist governance. They deviate by establishing different electoral bases—and consequent differences in legislative-executive branch loyalties and constituency-elected official relationships. In a *parliamentary* structure, the chief executive of government is the leader of the majority or plurality party in the most publicly representative chamber of the state legislature. The design insures a legislative-executive fusion in policy activity, and it denies the chief executive the ability to claim a personal governance mandate from the entire state electorate. Her or his immediate executive branch subordinates (Cabinet Secretaries or Ministers) are mostly senior and partisan aligned legislators. In a *presidential* structure, the state's chief executive is elected separately from the legislators and in a statewide election. He or she has greater authority in the choice of senior executive branch subordinates, and claims the unique status of holding the only statewide public mandate to exercise authority. Generally, *parliamentary* structures reflect a national respect for political consensus. *Presidential* structures more indicate national political diversity and a desire—by the electorate—to favor administrative decisiveness over consensus building in governance.

PLEBISCITE: Governance authority based on a mandate—often to one individual—from the governed citizenry. The implication is that the grant of authority is continually contingent on public approval.

PLURALISM (versus DEMOCRACY): In both environments, supreme authority rests perpetually with the citizenry. Yet, a pure *democracy* provides all citizens equal meaningful influence on all governance issues, and no populous and economically complex nation can achieve effective self governance through such diffuse structures and processes. A *pluralist* environment establishes and maintains institutions and processes whereby popularly chosen representatives of the citizenry address and execute the national policy agenda—each representative acting to represent his or her constituents. Periodic, public review of the representatives' official performances, with routines for replacement of a poorly performing representative, is integral to the *pluralist* governance environment.

PORTFOLIO (versus DIRECT) BUSINESS INFLUENCE: *Portfolio* influence over a private enterprise is intended as a means of profit accumulation only, from growth in the business's market successes, not as a route to controlling its operation. *Direct* influence or involvement constitutes managerial control over its operation.

The labels "predisposition", "trait", "characteristic", and "dimension" are used interchangeably in referencing attributes of a national culture.

REGIME (versus GOVERNMENT): A *regime* is an ongoing system of governance (constitutional monarchy, presidential or parliamentary system, etc.), whereas a *government* refers to one administration only within a regime (the Thatcher government, the Chirac government, etc.).

Index

About the Author

Robert M. Brown combines twenty years of experience as an active Army armored cavalry officer with over twenty years of teaching, research and writing about American and global politics. He has been on the teaching faculties of Boston and Georgetown Universities, Florida State University and both Troy State and the University of South Alabama. He received his Ph.D. degree from Florida State University in 1985.